Managing Employee Turnover

What People Are Saying About

Managing Employee Turnover

"Employees are a company's #1 asset and this new book provides keen insight into the myths and realities of managing employee turnover. As a business owner myself, I also really appreciate the tips on recruitment and retention that are vital ingredients to a growing business like mine."

—Jay B. Myers, Founder/CEO, Interactive Solutions, Inc.

"As a CEO of three manufacturing plants with over 1000 employees, monitoring and understanding employee turnover is one of my most important jobs. *Managing Employee Turnover* gives the tools based on facts to change turnover behavior. Allen and Bryant's evidence-based management approach is superb."

—Karl Schledwitz, CEO/Chairman, Monogram Foods

"An informative read, *Managing Employee Turnover* should be required reading for every HR leader."

—Gary Johnson, President, Gap Solutions

"Finally a book that offers evidence-based solutions for retaining talent! This is the definitive guide to employee retention for HR managers and scholars alike."

—James M. Vardaman, Ph.D., Mississippi State University

"This is a must-read for top level managers. It gives great new guidance on age-old Human Resource problems. As a former CEO of a public Information Technology professional services firm, I can say that I truly wish *Managing Employee Turnover* was available a few years earlier for me with my challenges of retaining top Information Technology talent."

—Ben C. Bryant, Executive in Residence,
FedEx Institute of Technology

Managing Employee Turnover

Dispelling Myths and Fostering Evidence-Based Retention Strategies

David G. Allen, Ph.D.
and Phillip C. Bryant, Ph.D.

Managing Employee Turnover: Dispelling Myths and Fostering Evidence-Based Retention Strategies
Copyright © Business Expert Press, 2012.

First published in 2012 by
Business Expert Press, LLC
222 East 46th Street, New York, NY 10017
www.businessexpertpress.com

ISBN-13: 978-1-60649-340-3 (paperback)

ISBN-13: 978-1-60649-341-0 (e-book)

DOI 10.4128/9781606493410

Business Expert Press Human Resource Management and
Organizational Behavior collection

Collection ISSN: 1946-5637 (print)
Collection ISSN: 1946-5645 (electronic)

Cover design by Jonathan Pennell
Interior design by Exeter Premedia Services Private Ltd.,
Chennai, India

First edition: 2012

10 9 8 7 6 5 4 3 2 1

Printed in the United States of America.

Abstract

When the job market improves, many employees who have had few options will be looking for new alternatives. Employee turnover can be expensive, disruptive, and damaging to organizational success. Despite the importance of successfully managing turnover, many retention management efforts are based on misleading or incomplete data, generic best practices that don't translate, or managerial gut instinct at odds with research evidence.

This book culminates volumes of academic research on employee turnover into a practical guide to managing retention. Turnover fictions are dispelled and replaced by research-based facts. Keys to diagnosing and managing employee turnover are presented such that readers can effectively manage employee retention today! These ideas are invaluable to audiences from CEOs who care about the impact of turnover on the organization's bottom line to the managers who suffer the most when their best talent leaves; from human resource professionals whose career success may depend on effectively managing turnover to students mastering new knowledge and skill sets.

Keywords

employee turnover, talent management, evidence-based management, employee retention, HR management strategies

Contents

Acknowledgments

As are most, this book was born out of the joint efforts of many. We would like to thank all of the influencers of *Managing Employee Turnover* in its current form. We offer the following list of names with a bit of apprehension knowing that some will inevitably be overlooked.

We thank the SHRM Foundation for supporting and encouraging our initial efforts to present turnover research in a user-friendly format.

We thank James Vardaman for coauthoring with us on the *Academy of Management Perspectives* (AMP) article that was the genesis of this book project. The 2010 AMP article, "Retaining Talent: Replacing Misconceptions with Evidence-Based Strategies," won two prestigious awards; thanks to James' drive for excellence and to the editorial guidance of Garry Bruton and Timothy Devinney who recognized the potential of the article and pushed us to achieve it.

We thank David Parker and the good people at Business Expert Press for believing that a couple of academics could produce an end product that's useful and interesting in both boardrooms and classrooms.

We thank those who reviewed and commented on early copies of the manuscript, including Ben Bryant, Jack Goldfrank, Gary Johnson, Jay Myers, Karl Schledwitz, and James Vardaman.

Denise Rousseau deserves a round of applause for giving her vote of confidence in our book by writing the foreword. Thanks also to Denise for blazing a path of evidence-based management literature that makes scientific management knowledge truly accessible to those managers who live it out daily.

Finally, we thank Heather and Dorothy for their patience and support as we worked on this project, sometimes at the expense of important projects at home.

David would also like to thank Rodger Griffeth for kick-starting his scholarly career and mentoring him over the years.

Foreword

Keeping employees who add value to the organization is one of the big three tasks in managing people. The other two are getting the right people to join and motivating them to do a good job. Research on employee turnover and retention dates back before the Second World War and has since grown astronomically. Professional managers, take heart. You don't need a deep dive through piles of studies. David Allen and Phillip Bryant have done it for you. What's more, they have organized the body of findings according to key decisions that managers face in managing both turnover and retention. Note that turnover and retention aren't quite the same thing, as readers will see. The result of Allen and Bryant's efforts turns science-based information into actionable knowledge to guide practice decisions.

A practitioner can get real benefit from reading this book in several different ways. First, you can read it with the lens of solving known problems—matters that might be keeping you up at night now. You will find you get a better handle on both why those problems exist and ways to resolve them. Second, read it with the lens of problem recognition—opportunities to make the current situation better by solving unknown problems. You will find yourself becoming more "decision aware," recognizing the opportunity for gains to be had through more deliberate action where matters were once ignored or left to chance. Third, read it to further develop your own professional practice. This means becoming aware of assumptions and uncritical beliefs that might block your approach to managing people or organizational problems. Our beliefs about human nature and assumptions about organizations develop early and often go unexamined. A goal of science is to help understand the world better, and a big part of that understanding is what we know about ourselves. Science does not provide answers, only facts to inform your thinking. In becoming an evidence-based manager, the most important competence to develop is your own critical and reflective judgment.

Denise Rousseau, Ph.D.
H.J. Heinz II University Professor
Carnegie Mellon University

Introduction

Racecars, Space Shuttles, and Employee Turnover

Employee turnover remains a critical organizational concern, and is likely to become increasingly important. Consider the following quote:[1] "Demographic shifts (aging populations, declining birthrates, economic migration), social evolution, inadequate educational programs, globalization, and entrepreneurial practices (outsourcing, off-shoring, on-demand employment) are between them causing shortages, not only in the overall availability of talent but also—and more significantly—in the specific skills and competencies required." Even with the down economy, retention among high performers has become more difficult due to budget constraints that limit bonus and incentive pay.[2] The Corporate Leadership Council reported in 2010 that 27% of employees considered "high potential" intended to leave their current organization, up from 10% in 2006. This suggests that while the economic downturn may have temporarily abated the talent crunch, competition for top talent remains fierce. Furthermore, as soon as labor markets become more favorable for employees there is likely to be substantial "pent-up" turnover.[3]

How can managers and HR professionals use data and evidence to effectively manage employee turnover and retention? When we work with students and businesses on understanding employee retention, one of our favorite activities puts participants in charge of a car racing team with an important decision to make. What does racing have to do with employee turnover? Even better, the case is based on statistics from a NASA space shuttle launch. What in the world (or out of this world) could the space shuttle have to do with employee turnover?

The case[4] requires members of the racing team to make a decision whether or not to participate in an important race when faced with the possibility of an important mechanical malfunction. Although the case is useful for numerous purposes, such as studying group dynamics and leadership, in this context we focus on the use of data to make decisions.

In the case, one of the mechanics is concerned that cold temperatures have been causing blown gaskets, and some data is provided on temperature and race results. Some groups ignore the data provided and just "go with their gut" (which is almost always to race). But even with the groups that try to use the available data there is a problem. They are provided data on the temperature at race time for races in which they have blown a gasket. Based on these data there is no relationship between temperature and blown gaskets—thus, almost all groups decide to race.

Why is this a problem? Because this approach ignores data on the temperature at race time for races in which they have *not* blown a gasket—by only studying one side of the outcome of interest, that is, blown gaskets, they are falling prey to a common decision making error—sampling on the dependent variable (or outcome of interest). When *all* of the data on temperature from all races is included there is a clear relationship between temperature and blown gaskets. This case packs additional emotional wallop because the data are based on information from the Challenger space shuttle launch that ended disastrously when O-rings failed and the shuttle exploded shortly after lift-off.

Duncan Watts discusses this widespread phenomenon as sampling bias:[5] a tendency to try to learn about phenomena of interest by identifying the attributes that occur when the outcome we are most interested in occurs. To learn about rich people or successful companies, he writes, we tend to try to identify the characteristics that rich people or successful companies share. Although this might sound logical, it ignores the possibility that less rich or less successful companies may very well share many of those same characteristics. The only way to really learn about factors that differentiate successful from unsuccessful or blown gaskets from not blown gaskets is to study both kinds and look for systematic differences.

So, back to the earlier question—what does this have to do with employee turnover? Well, how do most organizations try to learn about why employees quit? They ask the quitters! They conduct exit interviews, study the attributes of leavers, or have managers, supervisors, or HR professionals check off the primary reason each person is leaving. Certainly, collecting these data from leavers can sometimes uncover important information or patterns that can be useful. However, this approach suffers from sampling on the dependent variable—only collecting data from leavers while ignoring data from stayers. It may be that most of the departing employees say they are dissatisfied with their pay—however, it might also be the case that most of the employees who stay are also dissatisfied with their pay! If that is the case, although pay dissatisfaction may be important for other reasons, it is <u>not</u> what is driving turnover decisions.

Returning to our opening question, how can managers and HR professionals use data and evidence appropriately to effectively manage employee turnover and retention? That is the thrust of this book. Retaining talent is important to leaders in all types of organizations. The costs associated with losing employees and recruiting, selecting, and training new employees often exceed 100% of the annual compensation for the position.[6] In addition to these direct financial costs, losing employees can also lead to work disruptions, loss of organizational memory and tacit knowledge, productivity or customer service decrements, loss of mentors, diminished diversity, and even turnover contagion where other valued employees follow the leavers out the door.[7] Additionally, when tough labor markets prevent many employees from moving, get ready to deal with "pent-up" turnover. When job markets improve, many employees who have had few options will be looking for new alternatives.

Despite the importance of successfully managing turnover, many retention efforts are based on misleading or incomplete data, generic best practices that don't translate, or managerial gut instinct at odds with research evidence. In this book, we take an evidence-based management approach in which we synthesize volumes of academic research on employee turnover into a practical guide to managing retention. We intend for this resource to be valuable to a range of audiences, from CEOs who care about the impact of turnover on the organization's bottom line to the managers who suffer the most when their best talent leaves; from human resource professionals whose career success may depend on effectively managing turnover to students mastering new knowledge and skill sets. But first, we ask: what is evidence-based management?

Evidence-Based Management

Evidence-based management refers to translating knowledge and principles based on the best available scientific evidence into organization practice, enabling managers to make decisions informed by social science and organizational research.[8] In his book, *Becoming the Evidence-Based Manager*,[9] Gary Latham discusses the art and science of management: most management books focus on the art, based on the authors' experiences or their organizations' best practices. However, these experiences and practices may or may not apply to your particular challenges or contexts. Fewer books focus on the science of management: methods and techniques that have been supported with rigorous research, and thus are more likely to apply across different situations. A key component of evidence-based management is the integration of research evidence (the science) with experience (the art). Applying research evidence without experience can lead to neglecting important practical realities or the context in which the evidence is being applied. Relying on experience without considering research evidence can lead to neglecting new developments and changing conditions while relying too heavily on a narrow set of experiences that may not apply in new and dynamic situations. Indeed, we think most of us would prefer a heart surgeon who has performed heart surgery before AND who is up to date on the latest methods, tools, and technologies available.

Most managers get plenty of opportunities to develop experience. However, it is more challenging to stay current with research evidence for at least two reasons. One is simply time: managers are very busy and are under constant pressure to deliver results and deal with crises in the workplace. There is limited time available for studying research that may not be immediately applicable to day-to-day concerns. The other is that research evidence is often presented in a format that can be difficult to quickly and easily digest. The gold standard for quality research is publication in a peer-reviewed journal. However, the nature of the peer-review process often results in articles written with a heavy emphasis on theory and on describing in detail complex statistical methods, but with little emphasis on the practical application of the ideas or findings. For that reason, effective evidence-based management requires systematic reviews of research evidence that are accessible and focused on translating evidence into practical implications.[10] That systematic accessible review is one thing we intend to provide with this book.

Evidence-Based Retention Management

Can evidence-based management principles be fruitfully applied to employee retention? There is good reason to believe that human resource management, broadly speaking, is particularly ripe for evidence-based management. Denise Rousseau, one of the leading proponents of bringing evidence-based principles to the study and practice of management, suggests that, on one hand, many human resource professionals would have to answer "no" if asked whether they know the scientific evidence for any of the human resource practices their company uses; at the same time, human resources research is well developed, with substantial evidence related to many organizational challenges.[11]

Employee turnover is one such challenge. There have been thousands of research studies conducted investigating how and why employees make voluntary turnover decisions. However, many managers do not have the time or inclination to read and digest all of this research evidence, and find themselves relying on conventional wisdom or mimicking practices from other organizations. In a prominent journal dedicated to bridging science and practice, the Academy of Management Perspectives, we suggested several keys to developing evidence-based retention strategies: creating a shared understanding of turnover definitions, measurement, and costs; developing an understanding of underlying cause-and-effect principles affecting turnover decisions; adapting this knowledge to a particular organizational context; diagnosing specific relationships in your organization; and integrating these sources of information into retention strategies.[12] Figure 1 summarizes this evidence-based approach to retention management. In this book, we expand on these ideas to provide a systematic review to aid in developing evidence-based retention strategies.

We think we are well positioned to provide such a review. Taken together, we have been conducting research on employee turnover for twenty years. Much of this research has been published in the field's most rigorous and prestigious peer-reviewed journals. The research that specifically led us to write this book was sponsored in part by the SHRM Foundation, one of the world's leading proponents of human resource-related research, and has won several prominent awards. At the same time, the bulk of this research has been conducted in the field, with dozens of

Develop a shared understanding of turnover among organizational stakeholders
- Define types of turnover
- Develop a consensus for costing turnover
- Develop a shared understanding of the importance of retention

Develop knowledge of underlying principles and cause-effect relationships
- Organizational equilibrium and the turnover process
- Evidence-based predictors of turnover
- Alternative paths to turnover
- Job embeddedness

Diagnose and adapt to a particular organizational context
- Analyze turnover costs, rates, and functionality
- Conduct internal and external benchmarking and needs assessment
- Develop retention goals
- Collect data on cause-effect relationships
- Design retention strategies

Figure 1. Evidence-based guidelines for retention management (reprinted with permission, Academy of Management Perspectives).

organizations of different sizes, in different industries, even in different countries. We have had the opportunity to survey, interview, and speak with thousands of employees in many different job types about their turnover decisions. And we have had the opportunity to interact with students, managers, and executives in our classes, executive education, and consulting activities where we discuss talent management and retention.

Turnover Myths and Retention Strategies

This book proceeds with two major sections. In the first section, we identify five widely held managerial misconceptions about turnover:

- Chapter 1: Turnover Is Bad
- Chapter 2: Turnover Is All About the Benjamins
- Chapter 3: Turnover Is Driven by Job Dissatisfaction
- Chapter 4: Retention Is Simple
- Chapter 5: Turnover Is Out of My Control

For each misconception, we illustrate how it operates in many organizations; identify the kernel of truth underlying each misconception; describe what the research evidence says instead; and summarize key evidence-based practical implications related to retention management.

In the second section, we identify evidence-based retention strategies associated with seven key interaction points with employees:

- Chapter 6: Recruitment
- Chapter 7: Selection and Hiring
- Chapter 8: On-boarding
- Chapter 9: Training and Development
- Chapter 10: Compensation and Rewards
- Chapter 11: Supervision and Leadership
- Chapter 12: Engagement

For each key interaction point, we identify important principles, summarize the research evidence, and provide practical guidance for implementing retention strategies.

SECTION I
Turnover Myths

CHAPTER 1

Myth: Turnover Is Bad

Understanding the Real Impact of Turnover

Manager Green is worried. The annual turnover rate in his business unit has increased from 14% last year to 18% this year, more than a 25% increase. Being a proactive manager, he decides to develop a plan to address the rising turnover rate. Based on exit interview data, conversations with other managers, and his own experience, Manager Green develops a comprehensive plan involving retention bonuses, a market-based salary survey, and hiring a consultant to improve employee engagement.

Manager Green presents his turnover reduction plan to his boss, Manager Savvy. The first thing she asks is how much the plan will cost. Manager Green has learned that Manager Savvy always asks him tough questions, so he is prepared with a well-developed investment estimate: $200,000. Ok, Manager Savvy continues, how much is each instance of turnover costing the organization? Hmmm, Manager Green didn't calculate an estimate for that. The questions from Manager Savvy continue. What is the average turnover rate in our industry? It turns out the average annual turnover rate approaches 25%. Wasn't Manager Green at the meeting where the company leadership discussed plans for consolidating some operations? Some natural attrition is desired right now. How valuable are the employees who are leaving? Manager Savvy believes a new performance management system is encouraging some of the lower performers to leave and she'd like some data to show whether this is the case. Manager Savvy concludes by telling Manager Green that she agrees with him that retention of key employees is very important, but that she needs more data concerning how the increasing turnover rate is affecting the organization. Back to the drawing board!

Kernel of Truth

There is no question that turnover can be extremely harmful to organizations. If that were not the case, we wouldn't bother writing this book, and you certainly wouldn't bother reading it. Consider this quote from two noted turnover scholars regarding the impact of higher turnover rates: "Collective turnover can lead to undesirable outcomes because it entails the loss of firm specific human and social capital, disrupts operations and collective function, saddles remaining members with newcomer socialization and training, and increases recruitment and selection costs" (p. 360).[1] In fact, our recent research documents that decreases in turnover rates can be associated with hundreds of thousands or even millions of dollars in improved organizational performance.[2] However, that same research shows that sometimes turnover doesn't hurt organizational performance, and in over 20% of studies reviewed, higher turnover rates were associated with *better* organizational performance. To strategically address turnover and retention, the savvy evidence-based manager needs to recognize that all turnover is *not* created equal.

What the Research Says

People leave organizations for all kinds of reasons, and they don't all have the same implications for managing turnover. An adequate performer who quits because their spouse took a job in another state may have quite different implications than the loss of a star performer who quits to escape a stifling boss. Turnover research has focused on making several key distinctions in defining turnover, for example: voluntary–involuntary, functional–dysfunctional, and avoidable–unavoidable, as shown in Figure 1.1.[3]

With voluntary turnover, the individual employee makes the decision to leave the organization, whereas with involuntary turnover, the organization makes the decision that the individual has to leave. Most

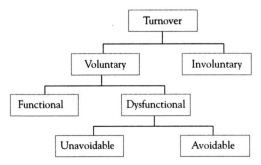

Figure 1.1. Turnover classification scheme.

Source: Reprinted with permission, SHRM Foundation.

organizations attempt to make this distinction, and the implications are quite different. In the case of involuntary turnover, the organization most often makes the decision either because the employee is not working out (e.g., violating policy, poor performance, or a poor fit) or because of organizational restructuring (e.g., downsizing). The assumption underlying involuntary turnover is that it is likely positive (or at least necessary) for the organization—or else why do it? Certainly, involuntarily terminating an employee for performance-related issues often makes sense, although we have seen cases where involuntary turnover was extremely disruptive. For example, one organization we researched was conducting drug testing and verification of a required state license months after hiring, and was terminating almost a third of new hires after socializing and training them. (Socialization is the process of learning about role appropriate behavior, cultural norms, and expectations for behavior in the work environment. Both socialization and training require investments in time and resources and losing out on the benefits of these investments can be costly.) There is also a growing body of research on the effects of involuntary turnover resulting from organizational restructuring.[4] Perhaps surprisingly, this research suggests that no more than half of organizations that significantly downsize perform better financially three to five years later. Thus, the proper management of involuntary turnover is important.

However, most turnover research has focused on voluntary turnover, because these are often valuable employees the organization would prefer to retain. Even within the category of voluntary turnover, though, it may matter who is leaving, why they are leaving, and where they are going. In terms of who is leaving, an important distinction to be made is between functional and dysfunctional turnover.[5] Turnover that is problematic for the organization is considered dysfunctional. Examples might include the loss of high performers, the loss of individuals with difficult-to-replace skill sets, the loss of hard-to-recruit populations, or very high turnover rates that are disruptive to operations. However, not all voluntary turnover is dysfunctional. Some instances of voluntary turnover may even be positive or functional for the organization. Examples might include the exit of low performers, natural attrition that meets business needs, or turnover that enables the organization to replace leavers with better performers, lower cost employees, or individuals with diverse new perspectives. Evidence suggests that higher turnover rates have a more negative impact on organizational performance in manufacturing and transportation industries; among managerial employees compared with employees without supervisory responsibilities; in mid-size and larger organizations compared to smaller ones; in the United States compared to Europe; and when organizational performance is measured in terms of customer service or quality and safety metrics.[6] Thus, the impact of turnover is not the same across individuals or contexts, and organizations can benefit by assessing the extent to which the turnover they are experiencing is functional or dysfunctional.

In terms of why people are leaving, one important distinction is between avoidable and unavoidable turnover.[7] Avoidable turnover is driven by reasons that are at least somewhat under organizational control. Examples may include turnover driven by job dissatisfaction, poor supervision, inadequate growth opportunities, or a negative organizational culture. However, even if an organization does everything right, some productive, valuable employees will still leave for reasons that the organization has little or no control over. Examples of unavoidable turnover may include turnover driven by trailing a relocating spouse, health problems, or winning the lottery. This distinction is important because it may make little strategic sense to invest resources to counteract unavoidable turnover. Another perspective on why people leave suggests that there are eight key types of forces or motivations that drive turnover decisions: affective, calculative, contractual, behavioral, alternative, normative, constituent, and moral/ethical.[8] We return to these forces in more detail in Chapter 3. The key point, though, is that designing evidence-based strategies for managing turnover requires having a clear understanding of why people are leaving.

Recent research also suggests that defining turnover requires expanding the criterion space by considering in more detail where people go, not just whether they stay or leave.[9] This research suggests going beyond simple stay or leave classifications and defining employee mobility decisions in terms of, for example, retirement, disability, death, firing, layoff, unpaid employment, an alternative job, a nonwork option, voluntarily staying with the organization, and involuntarily staying with the organization because they are unable to find a suitable alternative. It may be that these different types of turnover decisions are the result of different drivers and processes. Thus, more fine-grained measurement will provide more information for understanding the real impact and causes of turnover in your organization.

In assessing the impact of turnover, it is also important to estimate the costs and benefits associated with any particular instance of turnover. Estimates suggest that the total costs associated with turnover can range from 90 to 200% of annual salary.[10] Turnover costs can be classified into separation costs and replacement costs.[11] When somebody leaves, there are usually direct separation costs associated with managing this process. Examples may include HR staff time to process the exit and conduct an exit interview, manager time, costs for overtime or temporary employees to cover the exiting employee's duties in the short run, and accrued time off. There may also be myriad indirect or intangible costs associated with turnover, such as loss of organizational memory, teamwork disruptions, loss of productivity, or diminished diversity. There may also be separation costs associated with replacing the departing employee. These can include HR time, manager time, recruitment costs, selection costs, orientation costs, training costs, and even costs associated with lower quality, productivity, or customer service while replacements master the job.

As noted above, though, there can be benefits associated with turnover. For example, in some cases the organization may reduce labor costs by not hiring a replacement or by hiring a less expensive replacement. In some cases, turnover could energize the organization by creating an opportunity

Table 1.1. Voluntary Turnover Costs and Benefits

Separation costs

Tangible

    HR staff time (e.g., salary, benefits, exit interview)

    Manager's time (e.g., salary, benefits, retention attempts, exit interview)

    Accrued paid time off (e.g., vacation, sick pay)

    Temporary coverage (e.g., temporary employee, overtime for current employees)

Intangible

    Loss of workforce diversity

    Diminished quality while job is unfilled

    Loss of organizational memory

    Loss of clients

    Competition from quitter if he/she opens a new venture

    Contagion—other employees decide to leave

    Teamwork disruptions

    Loss of seasoned mentors

Replacement costs

General Costs

    HR staff time (e.g., benefits enrollment, recruitment, selection, orientation)

    Hiring manager time (e.g., input on new hire decision, orientation, training)

Recruitment

    Advertising

    Employment agency fees

    Hiring inducements (e.g., bonus, relocation, perks)

    Referral bonuses

Selection

    Selection measure expenses (e.g., costs of work samples, selection tests)

    Application expenses

Orientation and Training

    Orientation program time and resources

    Formal and informal training (time, materials, equipment, mentoring)

    Socialization (e.g., time of other employees, travel)

    Productivity loss (e.g., loss of production until replacement is fully proficient)

(Continued)

Table 1.1. Voluntary Turnover Costs and Benefits—(Continued)

Turnover benefits
Savings may be achieved by not replacing leaver
There is an infusion of new skills or creativity into the organization
Vacancy creates transfer or promotion opportunity for others
Cost savings may be achieved by hiring a replacement with less experience or seniority
Replacement could be a better performer and organization citizen
Replacement could enhance workplace diversity
Departure may offer the opportunity to reorganize the work unit

Source: Adapted with permission, Academy of Management Perspectives.

for someone else, by bringing in a better performer, or by infusing new skills, new perspectives, or increased diversity into the organization. See Table 1.1 for an outline of major costs and benefits associated with voluntary turnover.

It is also important to keep in mind that the impact of turnover is not the same for every employee who leaves, because not every employee is of equal value to the organization. Research suggests that some positions are more pivotal than others.[12] For many positions, retention is important up to a point, because high turnover in these positions would be costly. However, improving retention beyond a certain point may present diminishing marginal returns. For highly pivotal positions, however, improving retention continues to have a significant impact on organizational success.

Evidence-Based Management Implications

Turnover research clearly demonstrates that turnover can be good or bad. Here are several key points for savvy evidence-based managers to keep in mind to strategically manage turnover:

- Carefully define turnover. Turnover can be voluntary, involuntary, functional, dysfunctional, avoidable, unavoidable, pivotal, or not, and may result in very different effects on the organization. Managers and HR professionals need to develop a common frame of reference for understanding what turnover means.

- Watch for fuzziness of measurement. An employee is told to quit or be fired, and then classified as a case of voluntary turnover. Exit interviews reveal that nobody leaves because of their supervisor, but supervisors are conducting the exit interviews. These are examples of measurement errors that commonly creep into turnover data.
- Collect as much data as possible. Turnover rates by themselves tell you very little about the extent to which turnover is a problem. Evidence-based turnover management requires data on the performance, value, and difficulty of replacement of leavers; the reasons why individuals are leaving, where they are going, and whether the organization could have done anything to prevent it; and the relative costs and benefits of turnover.
- Develop a turnover cost formula. Savvy managers need to know how much each instance of turnover costs the organization, accounting for direct and indirect costs, as well as potential benefits. A consensus on the appropriate cost is more important than any one formula. Recognize that the formula may differ by position.

Final Thought

Turnover is not always harmful, some turnover is likely inevitable and positive, and turnover rates by themselves are not particularly useful. Effectively defining and measuring turnover and the relative costs and benefits associated with it are keys to strategically managing it. Returning to Manager Green, next time he will have data on who is leaving, why they are leaving, where they are going, and how much it is costing the organization. This will enable him to develop a more evidence-based retention plan, and to justify the required investments.

CHAPTER 2

Myth: It's All About the Benjamins

Understanding What Really Drives Turnover Decisions

Benjamin is troubled. Generally speaking, he likes working for the organization, but lately he's been feeling like his boss doesn't really appreciate him. Because of this, he is worried about his opportunities for advancement. Benjamin decides to start looking for other possible jobs. He currently makes $40,000 per year; thus, his job search only targets opportunities that make $40,000 or more. He would have to be REALLY unhappy to consider taking a pay cut! After a few months of searching, Benjamin finds another opportunity that pays $46,000 per year. After weighing the pros and cons of staying or leaving, he decides to take the new job. When his boss asks him why he is leaving, Benjamin says it is because he has found a new job paying 15% more. Benjamin's boss approaches Manager Green. She says that a valued employee is leaving because of his compensation; is there anything the organization can do? Now Manager Green is troubled. He would like to retain Benjamin, and the organization could probably counter-offer a few thousand dollars. However, Benjamin is already near the top of his pay band, and the organization is hesitant about setting precedents that encourage employees to seek outside offers for the purpose of leveraging counter-offers. Maybe it is time to revamp the compensation system! Manager Green approaches Manager Savvy to discuss compensation system design, but Manager Savvy asks a very insightful question: is Benjamin really leaving because of his pay?

Kernel of Truth

When we ask managers, executives, HR professionals, and students why people quit jobs, pay is almost invariably the first or second reason provided. It is true that some people quit because they are unhappy with their pay. It is also true that people often quit in order to take higher paying jobs elsewhere, although, as described in the example above, this can be misleading. Benjamin likely would never have been searching for that higher paying job if he had felt his boss was looking out for his best interests. It is also true that there are ways of structuring pay that can affect retention. For example, evidence shows that how widely pay is dispersed among employees affects the tenure of managers and the likelihood of their leaving the organization such that turnover is higher when the spread between average employee compensation and high employee compensation is wider.[1] We discuss creative ways to structure compensation to manage turnover in more detail in Chapter 10. However, the bulk of the research evidence suggests that pay may not be nearly as important as many managers believe.

What the Research Says

We reviewed the most up-to-date research summarizing the results of hundreds of peer-reviewed studies of predictors of individual turnover decisions (summarized in Figure 2.1).[2] Out of 41 predictors, level of pay was tied for the 30th strongest relationship with turnover. Ok, so maybe it is not the level of pay that matters. After all, some people might be quite happy and satisfied with relatively modest pay. Others might be very dissatisfied even with very high pay, especially if the person working near you doing the same job makes more. Evaluations of pay are probably relative. Surely, then, how satisfied or dissatisfied I am with my pay should be a better predictor of turnover? Nope. Out of 41 predictors, pay satisfaction showed the 35th strongest relationship with turnover!

Conclusion: despite the widespread belief that pay is an important driver of turnover, pay level and pay satisfaction are relatively weak predictors of individual turnover decisions. So, what are stronger predictors

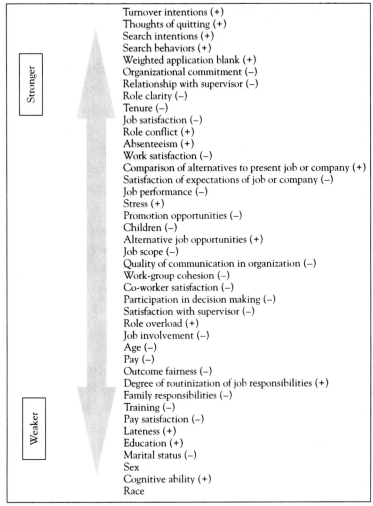

Turnover intentions (+)
Thoughts of quitting (+)
Search intentions (+)
Search behaviors (+)
Weighted application blank (+)
Organizational commitment (–)
Relationship with supervisor (–)
Role clarity (–)
Tenure (–)
Job satisfaction (–)
Role conflict (+)
Absenteeism (+)
Work satisfaction (–)
Comparison of alternatives to present job or company (+)
Satisfaction of expectations of job or company (–)
Job performance (–)
Stress (+)
Promotion opportunities (–)
Children (–)
Alternative job opportunities (+)
Job scope (–)
Quality of communication in organization (–)
Work-group cohesion (–)
Co-worker satisfaction (–)
Participation in decision making (–)
Satisfaction with supervisor (–)
Role overload (+)
Job involvement (–)
Age (–)
Pay (–)
Outcome fairness (–)
Degree of routinization of job responsibilities (+)
Family responsibilities (–)
Training (–)
Pay satisfaction (–)
Lateness (+)
Education (+)
Marital status (–)
Sex
Cognitive ability (+)
Race

Stronger

Weaker

Note: A plus (+) indicates that the predictor is positively related to turnover. (As the predictor increases, so does turnover.)
A minus (–) indicates that the predictor is negatively related to turnover. (As the predictor increases, turnover decreases.)

Figure 2.1. Voluntary turnover predictors.

Source: Reprinted with permission, SHRM Foundation.

of who is likely to quit? The studies cited above suggest three primary categories of predictors that are more strongly related to turnover: the withdrawal process, key job attitudes, and the work environment.

Research consistently demonstrates that the predictors with the strongest relationships with turnover are those related to the withdrawal process, notably turnover intentions, individual mobility, and job search. Although some individuals may quit jobs quickly and impulsively, most go through one or more steps of psychological or behavioral withdrawal first.[3] For example, individuals may experience thoughts of quitting, search for alternatives, evaluate possible alternatives against their current job, and develop intentions to quit, meaning they definitely plan to quit as soon as a preferable opportunity presents itself. Being aware of the importance of the withdrawal process is important for managing retention for two reasons. First and foremost, it allows savvy managers to intervene in the withdrawal process before it is too late. Discovering that a valued employee is leaving after they have found a preferable alternative and decided to leave is often too late. However, there are methods of measuring withdrawal process variables that would enable managers to take action before employees decide to quit. Second, there is considerable research evidence about the drivers of turnover intentions and job search, and the good news is that this research is quite consistent with the drivers of ultimate turnover.

Research also consistently demonstrates that key job attitudes, notably job satisfaction and organizational commitment, are relatively strong predictors of turnover and the withdrawal process. Job satisfaction is a positive emotional state resulting from the appraisal of one's job or job experiences.[4] Organizational commitment is the employee's psychological attachment to the organization.[5] Many organizations already measure these attitudes. If you do, good! If you don't, the research suggests that you should. Our experience suggests two key improvements many organizations can make in how they assess job satisfaction and organizational commitment. One is to be sure to use well-developed measures with substantial validation evidence. Many organizations rely on a single question to tap a complex multifaceted idea such as job satisfaction (e.g., an employee could be quite satisfied with their tasks but dissatisfied with their work environment, or vice versa) or make up their own questions without putting substantial research behind them. There are many excellent measures of both satisfaction and commitment available in the published research domain that have already been subjected to extensive testing and validation and are freely available. (Validation refers to the process of ensuring the soundness of a particular measure and for predicting outcomes important to organizations such as turnover.) The other is to measure more frequently and link individual responses to important outcomes. Many organizations assess attitudes only once a year, on anonymous surveys, with results only analyzed at the department or business unit level. Although linkage research of this nature has some value, we have found that more frequent assessment at the individual level allows for more timely and targeted interventions. There can be large differences between what is happening across business units and what is happening to the individuals within any given unit. This methodology requires building up substantial trust in the workforce and/or working with outside researchers to collect such data.

The next strongest class of turnover predictors includes key variables related to the work environment, notably aspects of leadership, work design, and relationships with others. Have you heard the truism "people leave bosses"? There is considerable research evidence to back this up. The strength of the relationship an employee has with their immediate supervisor/manager is one of the most consistent predictors of turnover. Research suggests that leaders help shape the roles that followers will have, and this process of role determination is called leader–member exchange (LMX).[6] This research suggests that leaders treat some subordinates as part of their "in-group" with extensive trust and access to resources, and others as part of an "out-group" with a more transactional relationship. Those in the in-group are substantially less likely to leave. Leaders made aware of these important distinctions in their interactions with subordinates and the subsequent impact on attitudes and turnover can better manage their relationships with their followers.

In terms of work design, research suggests that role clarity and role conflict are two of the most consistent predictors of turnover. Role theory[7] suggests that individuals hold multiple roles that come with expectations that influence behavior. When there is a lack of clarity (such as ambiguous department goals) concerning role expectations or when role expectations are in conflict with each other (such as having to report to two bosses with competing agendas), individuals can experience stress, burnout, and dissatisfaction, and are more likely to quit. Leaders and organizations need to ensure that expectations are clearly communicated and supported. The other element of work design that is directly relevant to the case of Benjamin at the start of this chapter is that opportunities for advancement are also consistently related to turnover decisions.[8] Individuals who believe that there are future opportunities for growth and advancement are more likely to stay—even if they are not completely satisfied with their present circumstances. Organizations would benefit from proactively managing career paths and opportunities, and leaders need to communicate with their employees about these opportunities.

Beyond supervisors, research evidence is also beginning to accumulate that relationships with others in the workplace are important for retention.[9] Satisfaction with co-workers and work group cohesion are two of the more consistent predictors of individual turnover decisions. As described in more detail in Chapters 3 and 8, employees can become embedded in a network of relationships at work that make it less likely they will leave. Managers can create opportunities for interaction and design work to foster cohesion. For example, research demonstrates that designing socialization tactics so that newcomers interact with other new hires and have positive interactions with experienced organizational members increases the sense of being embedded in the organization, which increases retention.[10]

Evidence-Based Management Implications

In summary, extensive research evidence on individual turnover decisions suggests several key points for savvy managers to keep in mind.

- Pay level and pay satisfaction are relatively weak predictors of individual turnover decisions. The use of rewards to manage retention is discussed in more detail in Chapter 10.
- Indicators of the withdrawal process are the strongest predictors of individual turnover decisions. Organizations should measure and manage employee mobility, job search, and turnover intentions.
- Job satisfaction and organizational commitment are key attitudes that are consistent predictors of individual turnover decisions. Organizations should measure and manage both satisfaction and commitment. There is extensive research evidence available for the savvy evidence-based manager on the drivers of these attitudes.[11]

- When measuring attitudes and withdrawal, organizations should use well-developed measures with validation evidence, assess more frequently than annually, and link individual responses to individual behaviors and outcomes.
- The nature of the relationship with one's immediate supervisor is a consistent predictor of individual turnover decisions. Organizations should provide leadership training to all supervisors and managers, and hold leaders accountable for retention. The practical implications of leadership for retention are explored in more detail in Chapter 11.
- Individuals with clear role expectations, minimal role conflict, and opportunities for growth and advancement are less likely to quit. Organizations should train managers on the importance of providing clear role expectations, design organizational processes to minimize role conflict, and develop and communicate career paths, especially to highly valued employees.
- Individuals linked by positive relationships with others in the organization are less likely to quit. Organizations and managers should work to foster positive relationships among co-workers, provide opportunities for interaction, and help newcomers form and develop relationships. The practical implications of socializing newcomers on retention are discussed in more detail in Chapter 8.

Final Thought

It should be good news that pay is not the most important driver of turnover. Revamping compensation systems, paying considerably above market, and throwing money at valuable employees can be complicated and expensive. Many of the recommendations provided in this chapter are less expensive to implement, more likely to have a positive impact, and thus, likely to provide a greater return on investment. Returning to the case of Benjamin at the start of this chapter, research suggests it would have been more effective and less costly to proactively communicate with Benjamin about future opportunities than to try to come up with a counter-offer or risk losing a valued employee.

CHAPTER 3

Myth: Turnover Is Driven by Job Dissatisfaction

Understanding New Perspectives on Why Employees Leave and Stay

Johnny turned and stormed out of Manager Green's office, threatening to quit as soon as he could find a job that would increase his paycheck. Manager Green sighed. Benjamin had already left, and the turnover rate in Manager Green's business unit has continued to creep up. Manager Green has learned that even though Benjamin and Johnny mentioned their paychecks, their motivations for leaving are likely deeper than that. Manager Green has also learned to conduct a much more thorough analysis of the impact of turnover. He has determined that there are two key subgroups of employees in his unit, experienced customer service representatives and project managers, who are driving the rising turnover, causing performance disruptions when they leave, and are very challenging and costly to replace. He has also discovered that employee exit interview data indicates that 70% of employees exiting his unit are dissatisfied with their jobs, and that job satisfaction scores from employee surveys suggest that the job satisfaction of customer service representatives and project managers has declined since last year. Manager Green is tempted to focus his retention efforts on job dissatisfaction; however, when he mentions this to Manager Savvy, she encourages him to take a broader decision frame before acting. Focusing solely on dissatisfaction of leavers and those in high turnover units could be a misleading example of sampling on the dependent variable, which is when you only focus on the outcome that is of interest as opposed to examining the complete set of possibilities (as described in the Introduction).

Kernel of Truth

It is true that job attitudes in general, and job satisfaction in particular, can lead to turnover. Many people do follow a "traditional" path to turnover in which they become dissatisfied with their job, or with some important facet of their job, such as the nature of the work, rewards, supervision, opportunities for advancement, or even co-workers. This dissatisfaction leads them to search for alternative opportunities, and to compare their current job circumstances to these alternatives. When they find an acceptable or preferable alternative, many people leave (although many do not). Some individuals even become so dissatisfied that they leave before securing an alternative. The most comprehensive summary of research to date finds that overall job satisfaction is one of the most consistent predictors of individual turnover decisions.[1] However, that same research suggests that job satisfaction explains far less than half of the variation in individual turnover decisions—meaning the bulk of the turnover decision is explained by other factors! Savvy managers need to consider additional perspectives about how individuals arrive at turnover decisions.

What the Research Says

Research is showing that job satisfaction may be a major driving force in less than 50% of individual turnover decisions.[2] Why do many dissatisfied employees stay, while some satisfied employees leave? We describe the research evidence from three key perspectives on turnover decisions that help to address these questions. One such perspective, the unfolding model of turnover, suggests that there are multiple decision paths that could lead to a turnover decision.[3] The unfolding model brings three key new ideas to the understanding of turnover: *paths*, *shocks*, and *scripts*. Research suggests at least four primary *paths* by which individuals arrive at a turnover decision that may each have different retention implications: leaving an unsatisfying job; leaving for something better;

following a plan; and leaving without a plan. We describe each path in more detail below. A *shock* is defined as an event that leads someone to consider quitting his or her job. Many shocks are negative job-related events that jar the individual into thinking of leaving, but all kinds of things can be turnover shocks. Shocks can be expected (e.g., graduating from school) or unexpected (e.g., discovering a spouse has to relocate); job-related (e.g., a negative performance appraisal) or non-job-related (e.g., pregnancy); and positive (e.g., winning the lottery), neutral (e.g., a merger), or negative (e.g., sexual harassment).[4] A *script* is a turnover-related plan that some individuals have in place that details under what circumstances they will leave their job, for example, when they finish school, when their spouse gets relocated, or when they earn a certain amount of money.

Leaving an unsatisfying job is the path most representative of the typical turnover process described earlier. That is, individuals become dissatisfied with one or more elements of their job or work environment, and then leave if they find a suitable alternative. Leaving for something better entails leaving for an attractive alternative, and may or may not involve dissatisfaction. This differs from the previous path because dissatisfaction no longer plays such a key role. Many individuals who are perfectly satisfied with their current jobs might still leave if they hear about or are approached about an attractive alternative. Traditional employee satisfaction surveys would not help the organization prepare for or intervene in these cases. These decisions may also be initiated by a "shock" such as an unsolicited job offer. Following a plan refers to individuals who quit in response to a script or plan already in place. Examples include employees who know they will leave if their spouse gets promoted, if they get accepted into a particular degree program, after completing a particularly marketable training program, or after receiving a retention bonus. These paths also have little to do with dissatisfaction and would not be captured by traditional employee satisfaction surveys. Leaving without a plan involves leaving as a reaction to a shock without a plan in place and without searching, evaluating alternatives, or undergoing the traditional withdrawal process. These are likely impulsive quits, typically in response to negative shocks such as being passed over for a promotion.

Below, we discuss some of the practical implications of these ideas, but first we turn to another key advance in thinking about turnover: job embeddedness.

Most thinking and research about turnover focuses on why employees leave. Recall, though, our discussion of sampling on the dependent variable: focusing only on leavers and reasons for leaving ignores something very powerful—why people stay. Job embeddedness theory focuses on the multiple ways in which employees become embedded in their jobs and communities over time.[5] This perspective brings two key new ideas to the understanding of turnover. One is that the reasons employees stay may be just as informative as the reasons employees leave. This is a powerful insight that provides a new perspective for thinking about turnover and retention. The other is that sometimes factors that have nothing to do with the workplace influence stay or leave decisions. These ideas may sound obvious, but they are rarely systematically considered in models of turnover or by managers. The primary premise of job embeddedness theory is that, over time, employees develop connections and relationships both on and off the job that form a network. To the extent leaving a job would require severing or rearranging these connections, employees who have many connections are more embedded in the organization.

There are three types of connections: links, fit, and sacrifice. Each of these connections may be focused on the organization or on the surrounding community. Employees who have more links, a stronger sense of fit, and greater sacrifices associated with leaving the organization would be less likely to quit. To the extent employees have links, a sense of fit, and sacrifices associated with leaving the community, they would also be less likely to quit when quitting would involve relocating out of the community.

More specifically, links are connections with other people, groups, or organizations such as co-workers, work groups, mentors, friends, or relatives. Employees with numerous links to others in their organization and community are more embedded and would find it more difficult to leave. Fit represents the extent to which an employee sees himself or herself as compatible with their job, organization, and community. For example, an employee who values community service would be more embedded in an organization and community that provided extensive opportunities to get involved in community service. Sacrifice represents what would be given up by leaving a job, and could include financial rewards based on tenure, a positive work environment, promotional opportunities, community status, or even home ownership in a tough market to sell. Employees who would have to sacrifice more by leaving are more embedded and more likely to stay. Interestingly, research is showing that job embeddedness is related to job performance and organizational citizenship behaviors as well as turnover.[6]

A third new perspective on turnover suggests that the motives that drive individuals to quit may be different than the reasons they provide (to themselves and to others) after the decision has been made. Summarizing a great deal of prior theory and research, the forces model identifies eight distinct motivational forces that act as the direct motivators driving quit decisions: *affective forces* (i.e., lack of positive emotional attachment to the organization); *alternative forces* (e.g., receiving an attractive job offer or believing in such possibilities in the future); *behavioral forces* (e.g., low costs of leaving the organization); *calculative forces* (e.g., low possibility of attaining important values and goals such as career development and promotion in the future when remaining in the organization); *normative forces* (e.g., wanting to be closer to family); *contractual forces* (e.g., breach of the implied contract between an employer and employee based on the mutual beliefs, perceptions, and informal obligations that exist); *constituent forces* (e.g., lack of attachment to coworkers and work groups); and *moral/ethical forces* (e.g., believing that switching jobs regularly is good and that staying long means stagnation).[7] This taxonomy of motivational forces provides a useful summary of the myriad predictors of turnover that have been studied. Further, the researchers behind the model have developed a survey measure assessing each of the forces.[8]

Evidence-Based Management Implications

Turnover research suggests that understanding and managing turnover requires a broader perspective than simply focusing on how satisfied or dissatisfied an individual may be with their job. Here are several key practical suggestions for savvy evidence-based managers:

Multiple Paths to Turnover

- For paths based on dissatisfaction, use traditional retention management approaches such as monitoring workplace attitudes and managing common causes of dissatisfaction and turnover.
- For paths involving better alternatives, make sure your workplace is externally competitive in terms of rewards, opportunities, and the work environment; also, be prepared to deal with external offers for valued employees.
- For paths involving plans and scripts, although it may be difficult in some cases to alter these directly, increasing rewards tied to tenure may alter some scripts. Also determining which scripts are common in your particular context may enable a tailored response (e.g., revised maternity and family supportive policies for large numbers of family-related scripts).
- For paths involving leaving without a plan, analyze the types and frequencies of shocks that are driving employees to leave, provide training to minimize prevalent negative shocks (e.g., letting leaders know how to provide negative feedback, minimizing harassment or perceptions of unfair treatment), provide employees realistic job previews and clear communication to minimize unexpected shocks or violations of implied contracts, and provide support mechanisms to help employees deal with shocks (e.g., grievance procedures, flexible work arrangements, employee assistance programs).

Embedding Employees

- To foster organization links: provide new hires opportunities for interactions with other newcomers and with experienced organization members, design work in teams, provide mentors, and encourage employee referrals.

- To foster community links: sponsor community events, and support community involvement.
- To foster organization fit: provide realistic information during recruitment, incorporate organization fit into employee selection, allow employees to sculpt their jobs to fit their interests, and provide clear communication about organization values and culture.
- To foster community fit: recruit locally when feasible, provide relocating employees with extensive information about the community, and build organization ties to the community.
- To foster organization sacrifice: tie financial incentives to tenure, and provide unique incentives that might be hard to find elsewhere.
- To foster community sacrifice: encourage home ownership through home-buying assistance, encourage employees to be proactive and involved in their communities, and develop career paths that do not require relocation.

Forces

- Incorporate the measurement of these multiple motivational forces into employee surveys and track changes in patterns over time.

Final Thought

One of the major barriers to effective managerial decision making is the tendency to use a narrow decision frame.[9] Narrow decision frames involve focusing on easily accessible symptoms and solutions to minimize uncertainty. To improve decision making, managers can broaden their decision frames by considering multiple objectives and issues, not only those most salient at a particular point in time, and by considering multiple alternatives, not just the first to arise. The latest thinking about turnover suggests managers should broaden their decision frames beyond dissatisfaction to consider multiple paths to turnover decisions and multiple motivational forces, and to consider why employees stay as well as why they leave.

CHAPTER 4

Myth: Retention Is Simple

Strategic Data Collection, Analysis, and Organizational Context

Manager Green is frustrated. One of his primary performance goals for the year is the effective retention of key talent. Following Manager Savvy's suggestions, Green collected extensive data using a broad decision frame to understand turnover drivers. He also developed a new formula for costing the impact of each instance of turnover, and has data demonstrating that he could save the organization millions of dollars per year by implementing a few straightforward initiatives that would cost at most a couple of hundred thousand dollars to launch. The estimated return on investment was almost immediately positive, and grew at a rapid rate over the next three to five years. When he presented his data and plan to Manager Savvy, she was impressed! However, the presentation to the executive team to get budgetary approval had not gone quite as smoothly. The CFO, in particular, questioned the cost formula developed by Manager Green and the likelihood that the interventions would work as planned. Based on the CFO's own estimate of turnover costs, plus the opportunity to hire replacements for departed workers at lower cost because of high unemployment rates, he requires significantly more evidence before approving the expenditures. Apparently, nothing is as simple as it first appears.

Kernel of Truth

Sometimes retention is simple. For example, we know that attitudes such as job satisfaction and organizational commitment tend to be related to turnover decisions. Other things being equal, work units with higher satisfaction and commitment will tend to have lower turnover rates, and individuals with higher satisfaction and commitment will be less likely to quit. Thus, paying some attention to job attitudes is almost always a good idea. However, dissatisfaction and low commitment do not always lead to turnover. Even when they do, this knowledge is not as useful without knowing what organizational or managerial factors are leading to negative attitudes in a specific context. Further, without a frame of reference for thinking about the impact of turnover, it is difficult to determine the appropriate resource level to invest in changing attitudes or improving retention. Developing an effective evidence-based retention strategy requires considerably more fine-grained data collection, analysis, and interpretation.

What the Research Says

Research suggests that a strategic evidence-based approach to retention management requires three broad foundations: (1) developing a shared understanding of turnover among stakeholders; (2) developing knowledge of underlying turnover principles and cause–effect relationships; and (3) diagnosing and adapting to a particular organizational context.[1]

Developing a Shared Understanding

Developing a shared understanding is critical because failing to do so makes it very difficult to design and implement an effective retention strategy. For example, if an HR manager believes current turnover rates are problematic, but the CFO believes the turnover rate is appropriate and an opportunity to reduce labor costs by hiring less expensive replacements, then it is unlikely organizational leadership will be able to agree on the appropriate investment to make in retention. Thus, care must be taken to accomplish three goals: carefully define turnover; develop a consensus for costing turnover; and develop a consensus concerning retention priorities. As described in Chapter 1, there are many types of turnover, and they don't all have the same retention implications. Organizations need to go beyond simply measuring turnover rates and beyond simply classifying instances of turnover as voluntary or involuntary. Instead, managers need to define how voluntary, avoidable, dysfunctional, and pivotal each instance of turnover is for the organization. To be able to do so, organizational leaders need to develop agreed upon definitions of these terms in a particular organizational context and provide managers the necessary tools (e.g., training, data systems, and resources for third-party exit interviews). Having these data available enables organizational stakeholders to form a consensus as to the extent turnover is an important issue to address, the appropriate investments to make in retention strategies, and how to focus those investments.

Similarly, organizations need to develop a consensus for costing turnover. As described in Chapter 1, there are numerous direct and indirect, tangible and intangible costs associated with turnover. Savvy managers need to know how much each instance of turnover costs the organization, requiring the development of a formula that accounts for the varied costs that may be associated with turnover. The key element of this costing formula needs to be that stakeholders throughout the organization agree that it creates a reasonable estimate. However, even in organizations that track turnover costs, the most common approach is to develop a single cost formula and apply it across all situations; thus, the average cost of turnover is multiplied by instances of turnover over a given time period to produce a turnover cost estimate. Unfortunately, this simple approach ignores the likelihood that turnover costs vary by position or skills, and that some jobs are likely more pivotal than others. Turnover costs will vary depending on who is turning over—losing higher performing, higher quality, more pivotal, or more difficult to replace employees costs much more than the inverse, and one size fits all costing formulae don't capture this. Organizations are likely to develop relative priorities concerning the costs associated with turnover in different parts of the organization. Thus, the turnover costing formula needs to be flexible enough to recognize and account for these variations.

Developing Knowledge of Underlying Turnover Principles and Cause–Effect Relationships

Another key to strategic evidence-based retention management is to help managers develop systematic knowledge about how and why individuals make turnover decisions. This is critically important because, as we have discussed throughout this book up to this point, managers left to their own devices often develop misconceptions about the processes and drivers underlying turnover. These misconceptions do not take root because managers are apathetic or unintelligent. Most managers are smart individuals who care a great deal about their organizations and the people in them. However, facing continuous organizational pressures and information overload, managers are subject to decision biases such as the sampling bias described in the Introduction. For example, one or two highly salient examples from a manager's career of losing a valued employee who leaves to take a higher paying job elsewhere can lead many managers to conclude that pay dissatisfaction is a primary driver in most turnover cases. However, we showed in Chapter 2 that this is a widely held managerial misconception.

How can managers develop systematic evidence-based knowledge about turnover and use this knowledge to aid decision-making? We suggest two primary strategies. One is for managers to learn all they can about the research evidence concerning turnover by reading systematic reviews. It is not necessary to read all of the research studies individually: there are numerous helpful systematic reviews available. One resource that summarizes much of this information is, of course, this book. There are also useful systematic reviews that can be found in key journals that bridge research and practice (e.g., Academy of Management Perspectives, formerly Academy of Management Executive) and publications of professional associations (e.g., SHRM Foundation).[2] These resources can provide managers a common frame of reference as the research evidence concerning processes and drivers underlying turnover decisions.

The other is for managers to make themselves aware of key biases that prevent them from taking a broad decision frame when faced with understanding turnover. As described earlier, managers are subject to a number of biases when attempting to draw conclusions about important events, and also tend to focus on easily accessible symptoms and solutions to minimize uncertainty.[3] Having a broad understanding of the evidence regarding turnover processes and causes can help managers to consider multiple issues and alternatives, not only the first or most salient to arise.

Diagnosing and Adapting to a Particular Organizational Context

Although understanding the underlying principles and cause–effect relationships that drive turnover decisions in general is an important foundation, effective management of turnover requires an additional type of evidence: the nature of turnover in a particular organizational context. That is, beyond understanding, for example, the roles of job dissatisfaction and shocks in turnover decisions, managers need to diagnose what exactly may be driving dissatisfaction in their organization and what shocks are most prevalent and important, and then adapt their knowledge of underlying principles to their particular situation. For example, one organization might find high turnover among hourly employees in a slow-growth market driven largely by a mismatch between expectations and reality; another might find high turnover among experienced professionals in a rapidly expanding market driven largely by disillusionment with career paths. The retention implications of these two examples are obviously quite different. The steps to context-specific evidence-based retention strategies include: thorough ongoing turnover analysis; interpreting turnover analysis through the lens of organizational context; and using multiple data collection strategies to diagnose the primary turnover drivers in a particular setting.

Turnover Analysis: Rates, Costs, and Functionality

Conducting a thorough turnover analysis helps to diagnose the extent to which turnover is a problem, provide data as to where the most important turnover issues reside, and encourage a broad consideration of turnover costs, rates, and functionality, not merely the most recent or most salient concerns (e.g., exit interview data about pay dissatisfaction). Overall turnover rates should be measured. However, it is more useful to also measure these data in terms of key categorizations that can help managers pinpoint the exact nature of turnover in their organization. Some key categorizations can include types of turnover (e.g., functional–dysfunctional; avoidable–unavoidable; voluntary–involuntary), job level, job type, performance level, geographic location, work unit, replacement costs, or demographic characteristics. Breaking the data out in this fashion enables managers to evaluate the extent to which turnover rates in different locations or among particular types of employees may be especially problematic. Organizations able to provide managers with real-time dashboards regarding these data will enable quicker adjustments and responses to potential trouble spots.

The next element is to integrate data on turnover rates with consideration of turnover costs and functionality. As described earlier, it is important to develop cost formulae that enable the calculation of total turnover costs and costs per incidence of turnover. Retention initiatives typically require investment of time, money, or other resources. Agreed-upon metrics for assessing turnover costs enable managers to strategically design and target interventions based on the best available evidence. At this stage of analysis, it is also particularly important to incorporate how dysfunctional departures are for the organization. Not every employee is of equal value to the organization, and not every position is equally pivotal to organizational success or equally difficult to replace. Recall our discussion of pivotal individuals and positions. In less pivotal positions, improving retention beyond a certain threshold may result in diminishing marginal returns, whereas, in more pivotal positions, improved retention continues to have a significant impact on organizational outcomes. Thus, a thorough ongoing turnover analysis that presents managers with credible evidence about turnover rates, costs, and functionality provides a critical foundation for strategically managing turnover.

Interpret Turnover Analysis Through the Lens of Organizational Context

It is not sufficient, however, to consider turnover data in isolation. Turnover rates, in particular, can be very misleading without a careful consideration of context. We have worked with organizations that would be thrilled to reduce their annual turnover rates in some positions below

100%, and with others gravely concerned because their annual managerial turnover rate was approaching 5%. The same turnover rate that is a source of concern in competitive labor markets or during periods of rapid expansion, might be considerably less of a concern during times of retrenchment, contraction, or high unemployment. The impact of turnover rates can vary depending on the industry, labor market conditions, quality of the current workforce, growth of the company and strategic plans for the organization. Therefore, the next step is to interpret turnover analysis data through the lens of your particular organizational context, considering past, present, and future conditions and trends both internal and external to the organization.

Benchmarking and needs assessment are two methods for assessing turnover data relative to internal and external circumstances. Benchmarking entails evaluating turnover data compared to both external competitors and internal historical data. For example, external benchmarking enables managers to determine whether a given turnover rate puts them at a competitive disadvantage with competitors in terms of talent and labor costs. An organization that has a significantly higher turnover rate than competitors, particularly among highly valued or difficult to replace employees, may be experiencing higher turnover-related costs, lower productivity, or service decrements. Conversely, evidence that turnover rates are consistent with or even below competitive norms could suggest that retention resources would be more strategically placed elsewhere. Internal benchmarking entails comparing turnover data to organizational trends over time. Often, increasing turnover signals greater cause for concern than stable or decreasing turnover. This may especially be the case if turnover rates are increasing sharply, or if turnover is increasing among particularly valued groups of employees or in particular locations. However, there may also be cases where stable or even decreasing turnover rates could be problematic, such as when the organization is attempting to downsize through natural attrition. Therefore, benchmarking and needs assessment data need to be integrated with consideration of organizational conditions and plans.

Needs assessment involves the consideration of future labor demand and availability based on internal and external trends. Internal needs assessment considers current and future organizational operational tactics and strategic plans that may influence the supply and demand for human capital of particular types. Some organizational strategies would be likely to increase demand for human capital in general, such as rapid growth in particular locations, growth in particular market locations, or for particular types of human capital. On the other hand, some organizational strategies would be likely to decrease demand, such as downsizing, retrenchment, outsourcing, or offshoring. The same turnover rate would tend to be more problematic and warrant more attention under expectations of increasing demand compared to decreasing demand.

External needs assessment considers labor market conditions, economic conditions and trends, and industry trends as they affect supply and demand for human capital. Some trends are likely to increase demand or restrict supply of human capital desired by the organization, such as industry growth, aging populations, shrinking labor forces, or migration of workers out of certain fields or educational programs. Other trends would tend to decrease demand or increase supply of human capital desired by the organization, such as industry contraction, growing labor forces, growing immigration by individuals with relevant skill sets, or migration of workers into relevant fields or educational programs. Trends that increase demand or restrict supply would tend to make a particular turnover rate potentially more problematic and in need of additional attention. Global companies may even desire functional turnover in certain low growth markets while they seek to reduce turnover in other high growth markets.

Taken together, extensive turnover analysis interpreted in light of organizational context provides extensive evidence concerning the extent to which turnover is a problem, and which incidences of turnover in terms of job types, locations, positions, or individuals are most in need of intervention. Further, the foundation of evidence on turnover processes and cause–effect relationships established earlier provides broad evidence-based principles for managing and reducing turnover in general. However, the missing piece remains context-specific evidence on why valued employees are leaving your organization.

Collect Data to Diagnose Cause–Effect in a Particular Context

There are myriad retention strategies managers could pursue, many of which are discussed in detail in subsequent chapters. However, managers generally have finite resources to devote to retention and must make strategic decisions about which initiatives and strategies to pursue. Further, some strategies are broad-based systemic strategies directed at the entire organization, large subsystems, or large subpopulations; examples may include improving the work environment, changing reward structures, or incorporating retention-related criteria into recruitment and selection processes. Other strategies are targeted at specific job types, work units, locations, or even individuals; examples may include developing a new career path for a particular job, or designing tenure-based incentives for particular individuals. Managers need context-specific evidence of the drivers of turnover in their organization. These data can come from a variety of sources including exit interviews, post-exit surveys, current employee focus groups, survey linkage research, predictive survey studies, and qualitative research. In most cases, multiple data collection strategies are required.

Exit interviews are widely used to collect data on why employees are leaving the organization. Often, a supervisor or HR manager interviews or surveys departing employees and asks questions about their primary reasons for leaving. Some organizations use third parties and collect these data after some time has passed in an effort to get answers that may be more honest or objective. Exit interviews serve at least three important functions: they provide immediate data on why employees are leaving; they can be used as a reactive retention strategy to attempt to convince departing employees not to leave; and they serve a relationship-management function in ending the employment relationship on a positive note.[4] However, exit interview data is subject to at least two major limitations. One is that many departing employees are more likely to identify external factors such as a new job and less likely to focus on internal factors such as poor management.[5] For this reason, some organizations rely on post-exit interviews or surveys, often conducted by neutral third parties. This post-exit data may be more open and honest than traditional exit interview data.

The other major limitation is that relying solely on exit interviews with departing employees is subject to bias from sampling on the dependent variable as described earlier. That is, it is difficult and often misleading to focus solely on data from leavers without comparing it to data on employees who do not leave. Thus, it is important that managers not rely exclusively on exit or post-exit interview data in developing retention strategies. However, given the multiple functions associated with exit interviews and their widespread use, we can offer some evidence-based guidelines for improving exit interview data: use neutral interviewers; train interviewers; develop a structured exit interview; emphasize confidentiality to the extent possible; and integrate exit interview data with evidence and data from other sources.[6]

To overcome the limitation of collecting data only from leavers, another data collection strategy is to conduct interviews or focus groups with current employees. These methods enable the organization to collect data from a representative sample of employees focused on identifying reasons employees have considered leaving, reasons they have stayed, and factors they consider most important for the future. These methods overcome the limitation of sampling on the dependent variable, provide new perspectives on why employees stay, and may enable managers to identify potential trouble spots earlier. These methods can also be focused on those employees the organization is most interested in retaining because of job type, location, skills, or performance. Similar to exit interviews, these interviews or focus groups should also be conducted by trained neutral parties and utilize a structured format.

Although useful, interviews and focus groups are time-intensive and typically include only a small subset of employees. Many organizations collect survey data in order to incorporate the perspective of many, if not most, employees. Survey linkage research can be used to link such survey data to retention strategies. The steps in survey linkage research typically involve identifying employee attitudes and opinions of interest; designing a questionnaire; measuring employee attitudes and opinions via anonymous survey; aggregating these responses to the business-unit level; and assessing the relationships among these employee responses, turnover rates, and other important outcomes such as revenues, sales, profits, and customer retention. Linkage research of this nature provides three key types of evidence. One, it provides data about the drivers of turnover at the business-unit level. For example, even if the employee survey uncovers that many employees are dissatisfied with their pay and their promotion opportunities, linkage research may show that only promotion opportunities are correlated with turnover rates. Two, it provides data that can be examined in terms of multiple subgroups that may be of interest, such as by location, manager, job or position, demographics, performance levels, or other factors. Such data may enable managers to develop more targeted retention strategies. Three, it provides data linking turnover rates to other business unit outcomes such as customer responses or profitability. Such data provides managers with additional evidence as to the extent to which turnover is problematic for the organization.

Although survey linkage research can provide valuable data about associations among many possible turnover drivers and turnover rates at the unit and organizational level, this approach only shows correlation, not causality, and does not help managers predict individual turnover decisions. Another data collection approach is to use predictive individual-level survey data in which individual employee survey data is statistically linked with individual stay or leave decisions over time. A valuable strength of predictive survey research is the specific data provided concerning the strength of relationships between specific predictors and actual turnover decisions in your organization. These data can help managers focus retention efforts and strategies, and may even in some cases enable early intervention to head off some instances of turnover before they occur. One important obstacle to consider with predictive survey research is that it requires a method for identifying individual employee responses so that these responses can be linked to subsequent turnover decisions. Unless there is a strong culture of trust and openness in which employees feel safe providing open and honest responses, it may be necessary to use outside researchers or consultants to ensure that employees can respond candidly without fearing reprisals from their manager or from the organization. In some cases, organizations use third party survey service providers that contractually preclude giving individually identified responses to the organization. In such cases, it may be possible to have an external researcher gather the data from the survey provider and the organization to analyze the individual level linkages and generate findings for the organization while still maintaining employee anonymity.

An alternative data collection strategy incorporates in-depth qualitative research that attempts to uncover the rich context and complex processes involved in making turnover-related decisions. Qualitative research involves collecting extensive narrative data from employees, often over multiple time periods, and looking for key patterns or themes that emerge in the way particular employees in a particular organization think about their jobs and organizations. Although often resource intensive, such methods can sometimes reveal issues or relationships not captured by survey research. Examples may include conducting and transcribing the content of repeated interviews with representatives of key employee groups; interpreting the content of employee journals or diaries in which employees are asked to describe their thoughts and feelings about the employment relationship; or experience sampling methods in which employees are asked to respond at regular intervals to short prompts asking about their experiences, attitudes, and thoughts about leaving at particular points in time. This approach provides great depth of information but conclusions are limited to the perspective of the people involved in the observations and interviews. For this reason qualitative data collection is often used in conjunction with quantitative survey research to confirm that identified themes hold up across the organization.

Evidence-Based Management Implications

In summary, strategic evidence-based retention management requires managers and organizations to collect extensive data about the nature and drivers of turnover in their organization, and to interpret those data through the lens of their organizational and environmental context.

- Carefully define turnover in terms of how voluntary, avoidable, dysfunctional, and pivotal each instance of turnover is for the organization.
- Develop a consensus for costing turnover, including flexible costing formulae by unit, skill set, job type, and location.
- Develop a consensus concerning retention priorities consistent with overall business strategy and economic conditions.
- Continually track turnover costs, rates, and functionality overall and by key categorizations.
- Develop systems that enable managers to track turnover metrics in their work units in real time.

- Study systematic reviews of turnover evidence and principles (such as this book!)
- Educate managers about decision biases and how to overcome them.
- Conduct external benchmarking to assess the extent to which turnover metrics place the organization at a competitive disadvantage.
- Conduct internal benchmarking to assess change and trends in turnover metrics over time.
- Conduct internal needs assessment to assess the impact of current and future organizational operational tactics and strategic plans on the supply and demand for human capital of particular types.
- Conduct external needs assessment to assess the impact of labor market conditions, economic conditions and trends, and industry trends on the supply and demand for human capital.
- Collect multiple types of data concerning the drivers of turnover in your organization, such as through exit interviews, post-exit surveys, current employee focus groups, survey linkage research, predictive survey studies, and qualitative research.
- Use well-developed survey measures with appropriate reliability and validity information available. ("Reliability" refers to a measure's consistency across time, location, and circumstances. "Validity" refers to the extent to which a measure adequately captures the intended construct.) A useful resource, the Measures Toolchest, is maintained by the Research Methods Division of the Academy of Management: http://measures.kammeyer-uf.com/wiki/Main_Page

Final Thought

Employee turnover can be a surprisingly complex phenomenon. Organizations routinely develop extensive metrics, analytical tools, and dashboards to help managers make real-time strategic decisions about managing all types of resources—decisions about retaining talent warrant the same kind of attention. Fine-grained data collection, analysis, and consideration of context can help managers be more strategic about using evidence to develop comprehensive strategies for keeping the appropriate human resources in the organization.

CHAPTER 5

Myth: Turnover Is Out of My Control

How Managers Can Directly Influence Turnover Decisions

Manager Green remains frustrated. Despite his best efforts, valued employees continue to leave and the turnover rate in his business unit continues to fluctuate. Many individuals seem to be leaving for reasons over which it would be difficult if not impossible for Manager Green to have any control, such as external job offers, trailing spouses, or even the employee who inherited a large sum of money. Even when it comes to the work environment, Manager Green sometimes feels like many aspects are out of his control. The organization announced plans to contract in size, leading many employees to be fearful and even to look for other jobs. Employee contributions to benefits costs are rising, leading to considerable grumbling and dissatisfaction. Manager Green is acutely concerned that once economic conditions improve and job markets become more favorable, there may be little he can do to stem pent-up turnover from occurring. He mentions these concerns to Manager Savvy one day over lunch. Manager Savvy shares some of his frustrations, but believes there are specific actions all managers could take to directly influence turnover decisions. She provides a few examples, and points Manager Green to a few sources he could go to for more information and ideas. After lunch, Manager Green sighs. It sure would be helpful if there were one resource he could go to and find a summary of evidence-based managerial actions he could implement to help manage turnover and retention...

Kernel of Truth

Sometimes managers may get frustrated by feeling that much turnover is out of their control. It is true that there are many factors that influence turnover decisions that are outside of managerial control, such as macroeconomic conditions and labor market fluctuations. It is also true that drivers of individual turnover decisions are often beyond managerial control, such as an individual who leaves to follow a spouse, to follow a script, or because of health reasons. Recall our discussion in Chapter 1 about avoidable and unavoidable turnover: there are some turnover drivers and turnover decisions that are unavoidable from the organization's perspective and it may make little strategic sense to invest heavily in trying to alter or prevent unavoidable turnover. Even considering many of the organizational drivers of turnover decisions we've discussed, it may be that individual managers have limited discretion to control or influence those factors. For example, if employees are dissatisfied with organizational communication, don't believe they fit with organizational culture, experience a negative organizational shock such as an announced downsizing, or are not embedded in positive relationships with co-workers, there may be little managers can do to directly influence these issues, at least in the short run. However, the good news is that research demonstrates that there are a number of specific actions managers can take that we can confidently say will have an impact on turnover and retention.

What the Research Says

Extensive research shows that there are evidence-based retention practices over which many managers have direct influence. For example, there are specific practices managers can employ from the earliest stages of new employees entering the organization that affect subsequent retention. There are even practices managers can employ *before* individuals join the organization that have been shown to affect subsequent retention.[1] One key example is that managers who provide job applicants the most comprehensive picture of what it would be like to work in a particular job and organization during the recruitment process can reduce later turnover. This is particularly true during the first year of employment, when turnover rates are often highest. Managers can act on this research in at least two ways. One is to provide realistic information to recruits about some of the more challenging or unpleasant aspects of a particular job or work environment prior to their accepting a job offer, enabling recruits to make a more informed decision about whether the job is a good fit for them. Another is to encourage referrals from current employees: research shows that recruits stemming from employee referrals tend to have better performance and lower turnover than recruits from any other recruitment source.[2] Many managers have even found the beneficial side effect that the referring employees also tend to stay longer after their referrals have been hired. Managers can also influence retention before hiring by assessing turnover predictors during the selection process. One way to implement the research findings on hiring practices is to go beyond selecting individuals solely for their ability to perform a particular job, and also focus on selecting individuals who are likely to be a good fit for the organizational culture and work environment. Another way is to screen for individual factors that predict turnover or job-hopping, for example, by using application information that is statistically weighted to identify biographical information that predicts quitting.

Soon after hiring, during the organizational entry and socialization process, managers can help to "on-board" new employees in ways that relate to retention.[3] For example, research shows that providing connections to others during the on-boarding process is related to lower turnover. Thus, managers can provide experienced organizational members as trainers or mentors to newcomers, and design socialization processes to enable new hires to experience on-boarding with others who are new to the organization. Research also shows that providing clear expectations about socialization processes and positive learning experiences during socialization relate to lower turnover. Thus, managers can design and communicate clear steps to the on-boarding process and provide positive feedback to newcomers as they adjust to their new work roles and settings.

There are also specific practices managers can employ to affect retention through the development of a positive work environment.

For example, research suggests that training and development opportunities can reduce turnover, especially when linked to tenure. So, for example, managers may allow valued employees to participate in valuable training programs or educational opportunities contingent on remaining with the organization for a specific length of time. Although we have debunked the myth that pay is the most important driver of turnover (see Chapter 2), there are strategic ways managers can use compensation and rewards to influence retention. For example, managers can strategically match rewards to pivotally important positions, hard-to-replace skill sets, or individual preferences; ensure the transparency of reward decision making to enhance perceptions that reward allocations are fair; and link some rewards to tenure. Research evidence also suggests that the nature of the direct supervision an employee receives can have a major impact on turnover, that is, people often leave or remain with bosses as much as organizations. Thus, managers can influence retention by adequately preparing the supervisors and managers that work for them in the science and art of supervising others. In some cases, this may involve holding these supervisors accountable for retention in their work-units or even removing ineffective or abusive supervisors.

Finally, an increasingly important element of a positive work environment is the fostering of employee engagement.[4] Engaged employees are not just satisfied with their work or loyal to the organization, but are energized about their contributions to the workplace and willing to go above and beyond their job description to contribute to the organization's mission. A key component of engagement is that employees feel that the organization cares about and values their contributions. Managers can design a work environment that fosters engagement through designing work to enrich job characteristics such as autonomy and variety, clearly demonstrating how individual actions and responsibilities contribute to the larger organizational mission, creating a challenging yet supportive environment where employees feel they have the resources they need to achieve challenging goals and will be rewarded accordingly, and other tactics discussed in more depth in Chapter 12.

Evidence-Based Management Implications

Below are some of the key evidence-based management implications that managers can implement to influence retention. We discuss each of these in more detail in subsequent chapters.

- Provide a comprehensive and realistic picture of the job and organization during recruitment through realistic job previews and encouraging referrals from current employees—see Chapter 6.
- Hire individuals who are less likely to voluntarily quit by selecting for person–job, person–organization, and person–environment fit, and by screening for biographical factors that predict quitting—see Chapter 7.
- During new hire socialization, design on-boarding to foster relationship building, provide positive feedback, and ensure clear communication—see Chapter 8.
- Provide training and development opportunities linked to tenure—see Chapter 9.
- Strategically design rewards to fit with strategy and preferences, enhance perceptions of fairness, and encourage tenure—see Chapter 10.
- Prepare, develop, and evaluate direct supervisors and managers to effectively manage and retain talent, including removing ineffective or abusive leaders—see Chapter 11.
- Foster employee engagement through job design, support and recognition of varied contributions, implementation of HR practices that encourage ongoing development and motivation, and drawing a clear link from individual contributions to the organizational mission—see Chapter 12.

Final Thought

Although many turnover drivers and decisions may be outside of a manager's direct control, there are many well-researched evidence-based

Table 5.1. Turnover Myths Versus Evidence-Based Retention Reality

Turnover myths	Evidence-based perspective
Turnover is bad	• There are different types of turnover • Some turnover is functional • Turnover costs vary
Turnover is all about money	• Pay level and pay satisfaction are relatively weak predictors of individual turnover decisions • Turnover intentions and job search are among the strongest predictors of turnover decisions • Key attitudes such as job satisfaction and organizational commitment are relatively strong predictors • Management/supervision, work design, and relationships with others are also consistent predictors
Turnover is driven by job dissatisfaction	• Job dissatisfaction is the driving force in less than half of individual turnover decisions • There are multiple paths to turnover decisions with different retention implications • It is also important to consider why people stay
Retention management is simple	• Context-specific evidence-based strategies are more effective • Turnover analysis helps diagnose the extent to which turnover is problematic • Organizational context matters for interpreting turnover data • Multiple data collection strategies enable more targeted and effective retention strategies
Managers cannot control turnover	• There are evidence-based managerial and human resource practices associated with retention • Section II identifies and discusses many of these practices

Source: Adapted with permission, Academy of Management Perspectives.

actions managers can take to influence employee turnover decisions. Table 5.1 summarizes the evidence-based perspective relating to all five turnover myths we've discussed. Although Manager Green's wish for a single resource that summarizes *all* evidence-based managerial prescriptions in one place may be somewhat wishful thinking, the remainder of this book is dedicated to describing how managers can implement many of the most well-researched and impactful evidence-based findings and practices regarding employee retention.

SECTION II

Evidence-Based Retention Strategies

CHAPTER 6

Attracting the Right Talent

Recruitment and Employee Turnover

Benjamin Schneider famously wrote that the people make the place.[1] Substantial research has followed up on his Attraction–Selection–Attrition (ASA) paradigm. The basic idea of this framework is that individuals tend to be attracted to and selected by organizations for which they are likely a good fit; in those cases where an individual is hired who does not fit, they are more likely to leave the organization (voluntarily or involuntarily). Thus, recruitment, selection, socialization, training, and turnover all interact to contribute to the organization's culture and the nature of the workforce. In this chapter, we focus on research linking recruitment practices with retention.

Among all human resource management activities, the recruitment process is the first formal opportunity managers have to manage employee turnover. Alison Barber has provided the following widely accepted definition of recruitment: "Recruitment includes those practices and activities carried on by the organization with the primary purpose of identifying and attracting potential employees."[2] To this, we would add that recruitment activities can also play the role of helping potential employees that may be a poor fit for the particular position or for the organization self-select out of the recruitment and selection process. Realistic job previews (RJPs) and employee referrals are both important recruitment practices that managers can implement to manage turnover. Both have been shown to enable organizations to hire individuals who are more likely to remain with the organization. Let's take a closer look at the research evidence behind the power of RJPs to help manage turnover and how you, as a manager, can get started with implementing RJPs in your organization today. Afterward, we will take a look at the evidence for employee referrals and how you can implement referrals in your organization as well.

Principle 1: Providing a Realistic Job Preview Improves Employee Retention

The Research Evidence

RJPs (defined as "the presentation by an organization of both favorable and unfavorable job-related information to job candidates")[3] can play an important role in attracting potential employees who are likely to be a good fit with the organization and discouraging potential employees who may be a poor fit. Much of the power of RJPs lies in the ability to provide applicants with accurate job expectations[4] paired with the applicants' degree of self-insight.[5] This occurs because of the voluntary nature of the job market. Armed with an accurate understanding of the job in question, a candidate with the insight to be aware of his or her own performance capabilities and career desires has the ability to opt out (self-select out) of a job opportunity that he or she perceives is not a good person–job fit. On the other hand, armed with an accurate understanding of the job, a candidate who is aware of his capabilities and desires is likely to more enthusiastically opt in (self-select in) to a job opportunity that he or she perceives as a good person–job fit.

In addition to the self-selection process described above, RJPs have also been considered by researchers to influence employee turnover through future met job expectations, role clarity, a greater commitment to their decision to accept the job, and enhanced perceptions of organizational honesty.[6] As a matter of fact, our research recently revealed through a meta-analysis (meta-analysis is a statistical technique for combining the results of many different studies into one integrated set of findings) covering roughly 17,000 employees that enhanced perceptions of organizational honesty may be the primary reason RJPs influence retention.[7]

Getting Started with RJPs

How can you put the RJP evidence into management practice? To get started, you should be aware of four important dimensions of RJPs—substance, setup, source, and sequencing.

The substance (content) of the RJP should include both rewarding and challenging aspects of the job.[8] Remember, you want to give a realistic preview of the entire job, not just a frightful warning about the negative aspects. Examples of rewarding aspects of a job may include a sense of accomplishment, a sense of purpose, or colleague camaraderie. Some sample challenging aspects of a job may include emotional trauma, high likelihood of burnout, or a fast-paced culture with multiple tight deadlines.

Popular setups (formats) for RJPs include booklets, brochures, videos, and verbal forms (such as conversations or interviews). Research has found that RJPs set up verbally, especially candidate interviews with job incumbents,[9] do a better job of managing employee turnover than do other forms.[10] General communications research, however, indicates that multiple communication formats may increase attention to and retention of information.

The source of the RJP is important for credibility. Future co-workers and job incumbents are among the most credible sources,[11] while professional recruiters and hiring managers (both of whom may be perceived as pressured and incentivized to just fill a job with the first willing and qualified candidate) are among the least credible RJP sources. Just as with format, though, general communication research indicates that multiple sources may increase attention to and retention of information.

The sequencing or timing of the RJP is also important. RJPs provided before a job offer has been made rather than after an offer can increase candidates' perceptions of employer honesty as well as increase the self-selection effect provided by RJPs.[12] It is also a good idea to pepper realistic job information throughout the recruiting process (e.g., in the job advertisement, the initial interview, the site visit, etc.) rather than viewing the RJP as a one-time event such as the delivery of a booklet or video.[13] This allows the RJP to be a more natural part of the recruiting process, allows for multiple communication points to ensure the candidate "gets it," and allows for the information to trickle in rather than blasting the candidate with information overload.

In Summary, a Good RJP Will:

- provide both favorable and unfavorable job information,
- include multiple formats, especially verbal,

- be delivered through multiple credible sources, especially future co-workers and job incumbents, and
- be integral to the entire recruiting process, not just after the job offer has been made.

Principle 2: Employees Recruited Through Employee Referrals Stay Longer

The Research Evidence

As a tool for identifying and attracting potential employees, employee referrals can be quite powerful. Research evidence has shown that job candidates recruited through employee referrals are higher quality applicants[14] and are less likely to turnover[15] than individuals recruited through more formal means such as newspaper advertisements or employment agencies. Three explanations for this include a realism effect,[16] a source credibility effect,[17] and a prescreening effect.[18]

Research suggests applicants recruited through referrals may be likely to possess more accurate information about what a job entails, similar to an RJP. Employee referrals may have an RJP effect in that the referring employee has an insider's (often first hand) knowledge of the work and work environment and is in a position to share this insight with the job candidate in an informal manner. A colleague once referred one of the authors for a position with his employer. Through a series of informal conversations, the colleague sent the message that, "you won't get rich working here, but it's a great place to work." He also provided insight on the manager and the department, insight that would not have been provided during the formal recruiting and selection process.

Having been friends with the referring colleague and his family for a number of years, I also viewed him as a credible source of information regarding the job. I put more stock in the information I received from my colleague than I did from the information I received from the professional recruiters for two reasons. First, I knew that my colleague would not jeopardize our long-standing relationship to fill a position in which he had no stake. Second, I knew the recruiters had a stake in filling the position and may be pressured to portray the position and the organization in a more positive way in order to fill the job.

Employee referrals also have a prescreening effect. The idea here is that a current employee is putting his reputation on the line by referring a job candidate and will therefore only refer candidates that are well qualified and would likely be a good fit for the position and the organization. The colleague from the example above recognized this and said early in the process that he would only refer me if I was serious about the position. He knew I was well qualified, but he wanted to make sure that his referral of me was not a waste of the company's valuable time and resources.

Getting Started with Employee Referrals

How can you put the employee referral evidence into management practice? The following seven rules of thumb generally apply.[19]

First, keep it simple but structured. An overly complex employee referral program is likely to deter employees from participating. No one likes a bunch of red tape. Likewise, an overly simple employee referral program is likely to elicit overly simple responses. A simple "do you know anyone who wants a job?" program is likely to produce an equally simple, "Not that I know of" type of response. In the case of employee referrals, Goldilocks got it right. Not too simple, yet not too complex.

A good employee referral program is rewarding but not so expensive as to lead the costs to outweigh the benefits compared to other recruiting sources. Employee referral awards are typically in the range of $500 to $3000 to the referring employee. The amount you decide upon will be based on factors such as the value of the open position to your organization, the typical costs of recruiting for this position using means other than employee referrals, organizational cash constraints, and other organizationally specific factors.

Good employee referral programs are more specific than unspecified. Being specific about the job qualifications and requiring employee referrals to meet those qualifications can increase the quality of the candidates referred by employees. It encourages the employee to do much of the prescreening for you.

Another way to encourage employees to prescreen their referrals is to limit the number of referrals they can make during a given period of time. Limited rather than limitless referral bonus opportunities encourage employees to be selective in whom they refer.

Rewards for successful employee referrals should be intermittent rather than immediate. It is generally a good idea to space the rewards out over time. For example, you may wish to specify that the reward for a successful referral will be paid out quarterly for the first year of the employee's tenure as long as the employee remains in employment.

The employee referral program should be communicated regularly rather than forgotten summarily. Like any other employee benefit program, it is not enough to include a short blurb on a one-page flyer received during orientation. It is important to regularly remind employees about the employee referral program and its benefits. For example, you may want to highlight cases of successful employee referrals in your company newsletter blog.

Finally, it is extremely important to ensure that your employee referral program breeds diversity rather than homogeneity. Because people tend to know and refer people that are similar to themselves, employee referral programs run the risk of limiting diversity and creating an overly homogenous workforce. It is important to encourage diversity in referrals and monitor the process for adverse impact.

In Summary, a Good Employee Referral Program Will Be:

- simple but structured,
- rewarding but not ridiculous,
- specific rather than unspecified,
- limited rather than limitless,
- intermittent rather than immediate,
- communicated rather than forgotten, and
- diverse rather than adverse.

CHAPTER 7

Hiring the Right People

Selection and Employee Turnover

Whereas recruitment's primary purposes are to identify and attract a qualified candidate pool, selection is the process of choosing the right candidate for the right job. In other words, selection is about fit.

Extensive research has shown that a person's fit with the organization and job can reduce the odds of subsequent turnover. As early as 1991, research by Charles O'Reilly and his colleagues[1] demonstrated that individuals who did not fit well in their jobs terminated their employment sooner, on average, than those employees who fit their jobs better. A decade later, Terence Mitchell and his colleagues[2] also found that "employees quit because their jobs don't fit." They reported that nearly 2 out of 5 employees quit because their jobs aren't a good fit. They concluded that the better the employee's fit with the job, the co-workers, and the organizational culture, the less likely they are to voluntarily leave the organization. Finally, a 2005 meta-analysis of 172 previous independent studies showed that an employee who fits well with the job and organization is less likely to turnover.[3]

You probably already intuitively understand fit in terms of asking, "Do this candidate's knowledge, skills, and abilities fit the needs of the specific job?" This type of fit is referred to as person–job (P–J) fit in academic circles and managers tend to do a good job of assessing it. But fit, in terms of employee selection, is a much broader concept. Amy Kristof-Brown has presented a comprehensive conceptualization of the many facets of fit in the context of the employee selection process.[4]

According to Kristof-Brown, a person's fit with the organization, or person–organization (P–O) fit, may be either supplementary or complementary. Supplementary P–O fit occurs when the person's personality, values, goals, and attitudes are similar to the organization's culture, values, goals, and norms. Complementary P–O fit can be either in the form of needs–supplies or demand–abilities fit. Needs–supplies complementary fit occurs when the organization is able to supply the needs of the person (e.g., financial, psychological, interpersonal). Demands–abilities fit occurs when the person is able to meet the demands of the organization (e.g., knowledge, skill, ability).

It may sound complicated, but there are ways to fairly accurately determine both P–O and P–J fit during the selection process by collecting what is known as biographical data, or biodata. Biodata are historical facts about one's life and work experiences, opinions, values, and attitudes.[5] Weighted application blanks (WABs—described below) and structured interviews have been shown to be excellent tools for collecting biodata (as we have broadly defined it) that can be used to assess P–O and P–J fit and ultimately predict an applicant's turnover propensity.

Principle 1: WABs Can Assess Fit for Improved Employee Retention Management

The Research Evidence

Weighted application blanks (WABs) are position application forms that include questions about one's life and work experiences, opinions, values, and attitudes that have been validated against performance criteria (e.g., turnover) and given weights in the selection decision process based on their ability to predict the criteria (e.g., turnover). Since as early as the 1950s, studies have consistently demonstrated the usefulness of WABs in predicting employee turnover.[6] An additional benefit of WABs is that they can be used to predict future performance on other criteria beyond turnover such as job performance, employee satisfaction, and success in training programs.

Getting Started with WABs

Research generally shows that WABs can be valid predictors of employee turnover and other important criteria when they are developed and used correctly, and that they are most valid when designed for specific jobs, although their predictive usefulness tends to diminish over long periods of time as the job, the organization, and their contexts change.[7] You will want to develop and validate your WABs for specific jobs within your organization and after you have implemented them you should revalidate and refresh them every few years. This is important for both strategic and legal reasons.

In developing a WAB, begin with as many items as you can think of that you reasonably believe are predictive of your criteria. Don't try to do this step on your own. A team of individuals familiar with the job including incumbents and supervisors will likely prove beneficial. If your organization has a good job description, that might also be a useful starting point. Try to think broadly about possible predictors. Some interesting biodata predictors of turnover that have been identified for military personnel include caring for large animals, camping, wearing associative logos on clothing, preferring country music, preferring group projects in school, playing chess, and having held previous paid job(s) supervising others.[8] The point of presenting this seemingly random list is to illustrate that seemingly random items may predict turnover. Just be sure not to include items that collect information illegal for use in selection decisions or that may be perceived as discriminatory or an invasion of privacy.[9] The same study that generated the above list predictive of turnover generated the following list, each item of which was also found to predict turnover: has experienced less trouble with the police, was a varsity football player, exercises more hours per week. Clearly, these items are likely to discriminate against the protected classes of race, gender, and disability. So generate your WABs carefully.

Now that you have developed the pilot WAB, you will need to validate it. The best way to validate your WAB is to have all new hires into the position complete the form. At a later date corresponding with the timing of your most problematic turnover, run simple correlations of each item against employees still remaining and those who have left the company. A simple t-test can determine if there is a statistically significant difference between the biodata on the WABs of employees who remain employed with your organization versus those whose employment has terminated. Correlations and t-tests can both be run using simple spreadsheet software such as Microsoft's Excel.

Once this has been done, you should validate the WABs using a new set of job candidates (cross-validation) to confirm they generalize across multiple job candidate sets. You can now implement the validated WAB items as an integral part of the selection process. It is a good idea to revalidate your WABs and refresh them as necessary.

In Summary, to Use WABs in Selecting Job Candidates:

- **Develop** biodata collection items that do not illegally discriminate against protected classes or appear as an unwarranted invasion of privacy (check with your employment law experts if necessary),
- **Validate** the WAB items by comparing leavers with stayers using correlations and t-tests, functions which can be found in simple spreadsheet software,
- **Implement** the validated WAB as an integral part of the overall selection process, and
- **Refresh**, revalidate, and revise the WAB every few years.

Principle 2: Structured Interviews Can Assess Fit Better than Traditional Interviews

Picture the following typical traditional interview. Behind the closed office door are two individuals. The nervous candidate sits across the desk from the hiring manager who has had little time to review the candidate's resume, or even the position description at hand. The two exchange pleasantries and the hiring manager fires his first question. "Are you married?" Not only does this question raise potential legal pitfalls, it is probably not valid either. Although seemingly inconceivable, one of the authors remembers the day he sat in the HR Director's office at a large regional bank. The Director began the interview for the position of Personnel Analyst exactly as described above. The unstructured interview continued with other questions not related to the job, including questions about kids, what part of town I lived in, and what kind of car I drove, among other uncomfortably irrelevant questions. The example above is just one from several traditional interviews the authors have found ourselves in. We've heard similar war stories from other applicants.

The other issue with using unstructured interview formats to assess fit is that this approach tends to lead to less reliable information on which to base a decision. Consider an interviewer who asks Candidate A primarily about their past job experience, Candidate B primarily about their leadership experiences, and Candidate C about their career goals. When the time comes for the interviewer to compare candidates, she or he will be comparing completely different pieces of information. Multiple interviewers complicate this further. Add a second interviewer who asks Candidate A about their educational background, Candidate B about their experience playing collegiate sports, and Candidate C about the one-year gap in their resume. When the two interviewers compare notes to make a decision, they will be basing their decisions on completely different pieces of information.

The Research Evidence

Research tells us that traditional job interviews are less reliable, less valid, and less legally defensible than well-crafted structured interviews.[10] The traditional job interview is often a one-on-one, undocumented experience led by an untrained manager too busy to take the time to craft valid interview questions. By contrast, a structured interview is a method aimed to ensure that each interview is presented with exactly the same valid questions in the same order by a panel of trained interviewers. These characteristics make a structured interview one of the most effective ways to assess an applicant's fit with the organization.[11]

Just as with WABs, important biodata type of information can be gathered in a structured interview. Murray Barrick and Ryan Zimmerman found several indicators that are predictive of both job performance and subsequent turnover.[12] These indicators can easily be ascertained through structured interviews. Predictors such as tenure in a prior job, number of jobs held in the last five years, motivation to obtain this job, intent to stay with this job, self-confidence, and decisiveness, are all predictive of future job performance and subsequent turnover and are easily adapted into structured interview questions.

Getting Started with Structured Interviews

Several good guides to developing structured interviews exist.[13] What follows is largely based on the United States Office of Personnel Management's 2008 guide to structured interviews. The following eight steps are recommended to getting started with structured interviews:[14] (1) conduct a job analysis, (2) determine the competencies to be assessed, (3) develop the interview questions, (4) develop the scales by which to evaluate candidates, (5) create interview probes if necessary, (6) pilot the test questions, (7) create an interviewers' guide and train interviewers, and (8) document the development process, implement the structured interviews as an integral part of the selection process, and monitor for effectiveness.

A job analysis will identify the job requirements and the necessary knowledge, skills, and abilities (KSAs) to perform the job. If job analyses have already been conducted, now is a good time to get your internal subject matter experts to validate their veracity. You want to make sure that the structured interviews will be based on an accurate understanding of the job.

Now that you have a valid job analysis, you will want to determine which job competencies will be assessed by the structured interview and how they will be measured. The guide produced by the Office of Personnel Management suggests that between four and six competencies are usually measured by the structured interview. Some competencies, such as oral skills, interpersonal skills, and logical thinking skills lend themselves well to measurement via structured interviews. Other competencies will likely be better measured by other selection tests (for instance, decision-making skills may be better assessed through a job simulation or in-basket exercises).

Next, you will want to develop the interview questions. Structured interview questions can take two basic forms. Behavioral questions ask about past performance and behaviors in certain types of work environments and scenarios. Situational questions ask about behaviors and actions the candidate would undertake given certain hypothetical situations. Either or both of the question types are good to use in structured interviews, although behavioral questions focus on applicant experiences, while situational questions focus on potential. Regardless of which format is chosen, the questions should be clear and concise open-ended questions that reflect the competencies discovered in the job analysis.

The next step is to develop the evaluation scales. The subject matter experts who developed the questions should also develop sample answers that represent competency levels along a rating spectrum that ranges from "does not at all display the competency" to "displays very high levels of the competency."

It is a good idea to also develop probes for the interview questions incase candidates have a hard time answering the question or their answers require clarification. Probes are follow-up statements that the interview panel can use to assist in cases such as the above. If probes are necessary, they should be used consistently across all candidates.

You are now ready to pilot test the structured interview on colleagues. This is the time to work out the kinks and improve the interview questions and sample answers. Now is also the time to make sure the questions are job relevant and are not discriminatory, offensive, or an invasion of privacy.

Now that you have developed and piloted your structured interview, it is time to develop an interviewer's guide and to train the interviewers. The interviewer's guide should include the test questions, the proficiencies they are designed to measure, the sample answers along with an explanation of the rating system, and any question probes that may have been developed. It should also include a brief summary of the benefits of structured interviewing over traditional interviewing as well as the importance of following the interview protocol.

To finish up, you need to document the process used to develop the structured interview, implement it within the selection process, and monitor it for effectiveness.

In Summary, to get Started with Structured Interviews in Selecting Job Candidates:

- conduct a job analysis,
- determine the competencies to be assessed,
- develop the interview questions,

- develop the scales by which to evaluate candidates,
- create interview probes if necessary,
- pilot the test questions,
- create an interviewers' guide and train interviewers, and
- document, implement, and monitor for effectiveness.

CHAPTER 8

On-Boarding

Socialization and Employee Turnover

Even with a realistic job preview and good fit, newly hired employees usually find the first few weeks at a new job stressful. There's a new job with new processes to learn and new faces with new names to remember. There are new rules, a new culture, and new politics. There are new benefits, a new pay structure, a new environment, and a new boss to impress.

Your company may already have a program for new hire orientation that covers benefits and job expectations. But is your current program helping you manage employee turnover? Socialization practices—the methods organizations use to help newcomers adapt to their new work environment, reduce the anxiety associated with starting a new job, and acquire the desired culture and collected knowledge of the organization[1]—are important to a new hire's subsequent tenure with the organization. There are six dimensions of the new hire socialization process that you can manage to maximize employee retention management.[2] These six dimensions, which are discussed and explored in the following six principles, have been shown to reduce employee turnover, mostly through on-the-job embeddedness (as discussed in Chapter 3).[3] When you are considering socialization practices, don't leave out your telecommuting and distant employees. Their physical absence from other employees makes them even more prone to feel left out and less embedded in the organization. Carefully consider what the following principles imply for all of your newcomer employees, especially the telecommuters and distant employees.

Principle 1: Formal Socialization Opportunities Can Help Reduce Employee Turnover

With *formal* socialization practices, new hires are segregated into clearly defined socialization activities while they learn their roles. In contrast, *informal* socialization practices are characterized by on-the-job learning activities that are not clearly defined as part of the socialization process. Formal socialization tactics may help your organization reduce turnover among new hires.

The Research Evidence

Our research has shown that formal socialization practices reduce newcomer anxiety and uncertainty by providing them with a consistent message. This consistent message may also lead to shared values among newcomers that fit the culture and values of the overall organization. Formal socialization practices also send a signal to new hires about the importance of adapting to the new environment.[4]

Getting Started with Providing Formal Socialization Opportunities

To recognize the full effects of formalizing socialization practices, segregate new hires into activities set apart from day to day, ongoing work activities. This may involve activities such as offsite training, new hire luncheons, etc. Pay particular attention to the messages conveyed in formal socialization. Messages that inform the new hires about company culture, values, roles, and goals are of particular importance. Ensure that these messages are consistent across all socialization agents and socialization activities as well as back at the work site.

Principle 2: Collective Socialization Opportunities Can Help Reduce Employee Turnover

With *collective* socialization practices, new hires are grouped into cohorts that experience common socialization activities together. This is in contrast to *individual* socialization practices, where new hires experience socialization practices alone. Collective socialization practices may help your organization reduce turnover among new hires.

The Research Evidence

New hires often feel displaced and out of touch. They generally come into their new environment from a previous work environment where they felt at least partially embedded. A feeling of acceptance and being a part of the organization is important to new hires.[5] Our research has shown that collective socialization can increase new hires' feelings of belongingness as they experience the new organization together. This heightened sense of belongingness is associated with greater on-the-job embeddedness, an antecedent to reduced employee turnover.[6] Collective socialization practices may also increase the links and social ties with others in the organization, thus making it more difficult to consider leaving the organization in the future.[7]

Getting Started with Collective Socialization Opportunities

To get started with collective socialization practices, organize new hires into cohorts that are hired around the same time and that are likely to work closely together once on the job. This will allow new hires to develop a sense of identity within the company and a sense of unity among themselves and can begin building the valuable social contacts they will need on the job. It can also provide needed social support from peers who are experiencing the same stage of acclimation to the new environment. Another tactic is to take advantage of social technologies to form online affinity groups or resource sites that enable new hires to share their experiences with one another.

Principle 3: Sequential Socialization Opportunities Can Help Reduce Employee Turnover

With *sequential* socialization practices, the sequence of socialization experiences and activities are defined and clearly communicated. By contrast, *random* socialization practices are characterized by an unknown sequence of events. Socialization practices that are sequential in nature can increase new hire retention by reducing their levels of anxiety and stress.

The Research Evidence

There are many unknowns in starting a new job that can increase the anxiety and stress levels experienced by new hires. Sequential socialization practices can add some much needed predictability to the crucial first few weeks on the job. Allowing the newcomer some control over the sequenced events may also add a sense of personal control over their new and uncertain environment.[8] This may be done by establishing milestones (such as passing a training course) that the employee must accomplish before moving on to the next step. This technique can also help new hires establish routines as well as gain a sense of understanding of their role in the organization.

We once worked with a business unit that was experiencing 80% turnover. The majority of employees were leaving before they had completed their first 90 days. We implemented a sequential socialization process that included three levels of new hire training, each of which culminated in increased prestige, increased job responsibilities, and a higher pay rate. Once the process was in place, new hires reported a greater sense of control over their career and of their own role in the organization. Subsequently, turnover in the division was reduced to **less than 20%** and sequential socialization practices were implemented across the company.

Getting Started with Sequential Socialization Opportunities

To get started with sequential socialization practices, make sure that expectations for progressing oversteps along the way are clearly communicated. This can reduce the stress and anxiety associated with the perceived chaos that often comes with starting a new job. Giving employees a level of control over the ability to pass from one milestone to the next can also be beneficial in generating a sense of self-efficacy (feelings of job mastery) and ability to succeed in their new role.[9]

Principle 4: Fixed Socialization Practices Can Help Reduce Employee Turnover

With *fixed* socialization practices the timing of progressing through socialization stages is predetermined and communicated to new hires whereas with *variable* socialization practices the timing is unknown. This is similar and related to the sequential socialization practices just discussed. The difference though is that with sequential practices the socialization stages may be known, but the timing of such stages may be unknown. However, with fixed socialization practices the timing of events is known. Like sequential socialization practices, fixed socialization practices may also reduce employee turnover by reducing anxiety and uncertainty among newcomers.

The Research Evidence

Like sequential practices, fixed practices can help clarify the new hire's role in the organization as well as the time that will be required to become a full-fledged insider.[10] To the extent that completing steps throughout the socialization process is related to greater status within the organization, fixed and sequential practices may elicit a greater sense of belongingness and ease of integrating into the organizational community. Finally, the timetable associated with fixed socialization practices reminds new hires of the time they have put into the process of becoming a fully accepted organizational member. This sacrifice of time put into the organization may also make the prospects of leaving and starting over anew with a different organization less appealing.

Getting Started with Fixed Socialization Opportunities

To get started with fixed socialization practices clearly identify and communicate the timing of the stages within the socialization process to new hires. Pausing to celebrate promotions across the various socialization stages can effectively anchor the milestones (along with the sacrifices, status, and acceptance associated with each milestone). This can provide the new hire with a sense of sacrifice, accomplishment, and belongingness that will make voluntarily leaving the organization less appealing.

Principle 5: Serial Socialization Opportunities Can Help Reduce Employee Turnover

Serial socialization practices include experienced organizational insiders as mentors in the socialization process. By contrast, *disjunctive* socialization practices do not involve experienced organizational insiders in the process. Research evidence indicates that serial socialization practices may help you reduce employee turnover.

The Research Evidence

Serial socialization practices allow new hires to begin building relationships with experienced organizational insiders. These relationships allow the new hires to start building important networks within the organization that increase their embeddedness on the job. This embeddedness builds a sense of belongingness and reduces the attractiveness of severing these ties by voluntarily leaving the organization.[11]

Additionally, experienced role models and mentors can help new hires make sense of their new environment during the socialization period, which reduces anxiety and uncertainty and increases the new hire's sense of the organization being a good long-term fit.[12] Both decrease the attractiveness of voluntarily leaving the organization.

Getting Started with Serial Socialization Opportunities

To get started with serial socialization practices, choose experienced organizational insiders who are sociable and politically savvy organizational leaders. Social, outgoing mentors lead newcomers to associate a sense of friendliness with the organization. Politically savvy mentors can be of great assistance to new hires as they try to navigate through their new unfamiliar environment. When high-level organizational leaders actively participate in the socialization process, it signals that the new hires and their acclimation into the new environment are of utmost importance to the entire organization.

Principle 6: Investiture Socialization Opportunities Can Help Reduce Employee Turnover

Investiture socialization practices provide newcomers with positive social support and feedback, while *divestiture* socialization practices provide more negative feedback during the adaptation stage. Divestiture practices have their place in strong organizational cultures where conformity and rule following are important. Divestiture is most commonly used in military or similar settings. However, in the majority of organizations, investiture socialization practices generally yield fewer turnovers among new hires.

The Research Evidence

Research has shown that the positive feedback associated with investiture socialization tactics is associated with an increased sense of competence and confidence.[13] This increased self-assurance, or self-efficacy, can provide newcomers with the confidence they need to stay with the job through the hard times.[14] The early positive interactions with insiders provided by investiture socialization practices facilitate organizational adjustment and fit among newcomers as well.[15] Finally, the social networks developed when organizational insiders provide newcomers with positive feedback have been shown to build a greater sense of community. All of these benefits of investiture socialization practices can reduce turnover intentions and subsequent turnover of new hires.

Getting Started with Investiture Socialization Opportunities

To get started with investiture socialization practices, provide ample opportunities for the success of newcomers followed by positive feedback from organizational insiders. Providing at least some of this positive feedback in social situations can enhance the sense of community among newcomers. This sense of community will encourage newcomers to stay with the organization.

In Summary, Socialization Practices Can Help Manage Employee Turnover When They Are:

- **Formal**—clearly defined, set-apart socialization activities,
- **Collective**—common, cohort-centered learning experiences,
- **Sequential**—the sequence of activities is set and clearly communicated,
- **Fixed**—the timing of learning activities is set and clearly communicated,
- **Serial**—experienced organizational insiders act as role models, and
- **Investitive**—positive feedback and social support are provided.

CHAPTER 9

Developing Human Capital

Training, Development, and Employee Turnover

When it comes to turnover, making investments in training and development can be a double-edged sword. Many managers fear that investments in training will make employees more mobile and, therefore, more attractive to other employers. Some evidence does show that if not handled correctly, investments in training and development may very well be investments made toward a competitor's future workforce.[1] Most of the evidence also shows that strategic investments in training and development can pay off in terms of an improved workforce and reduced turnover.[2] Besides, when managers express concern about what happens if the organization trains everyone and they all leave, we like to offer the alternative that the organization fails to train anyone and they all stay!

The link between training and development and turnover should be viewed in terms of career development.[3] In the traditional psychological contract (a psychological contract represents the shared beliefs, perceptions, and common understanding of informal obligations between an employer and an employee) that was held between an employer and its employees throughout most of the 20th century, the employer offered relatively long-term, stable employment in return for satisfactory job performance and positive organizational citizenship. In the current century, the psychological contract has changed. Employers are now expecting above average performance but no longer imply the availability of long-term employment. Employees, especially high performers, now expect in return for their efforts for the organization, the opportunity to grow, develop, and advance their careers.[4] A 2010 survey conducted by Robert Grossman, lawyer and professor of management, discovered that one quarter of high potential employees planned to change jobs within the next 12 months. Of these high potential employees eager to move on, 64% confided that their current employment situation was not providing for their career development needs.[5] The implication is that at least some of these high potential employees may be less likely to consider changing jobs if their current employers offered greater training and development opportunities.

High performing and high potential employees today value what has been termed career adaptability. They want their employer to provide them with the developmental opportunities they need to advance their career, whether that means remaining with their current employer or moving on. Ito and Brotheridge[6] found evidence for the resulting paradox—career adaptability is positively correlated with **both** organizational commitment **and** intentions to leave. This means that managers must provide employees with **both** development opportunities **and** the advancement opportunities that match their individual career goals.

The following four principles are discussed further in the remainder of this chapter:

(1) Managers should know that, in general, providing employees with training and development opportunities reduces their propensity to turnover. (2) Less market mobility is associated with more job specific training and development. This creates a low turnover environment when coupled with internal career advancement opportunities. (3) Tying training and development opportunities to tenure requirements may encourage employees to stay longer. (4) Training supervisors and managers, especially in effective leadership and management skills, can reduce turnover among frontline employees and supervisors and managers.

Principle 1: Providing Training and Development Opportunities Can Reduce Employee Turnover

The Research Evidence

Training and development opportunities tend to reduce the desire to leave an organization.[7] One possible reason for this is that it increases employees' perceptions that the organization is supportive of them.

This increases their overall job satisfaction, which in turn decreases their desire to leave. This was the relationship observed by Karl Pajo and his colleagues.[8] In their 2010 *Journal of Small Business Management* article, they stress that this link between training and development and reduced turnover is entirely dependent upon the intermediate responses of perceived organizational support and job satisfaction. The implication is that if employees have reason to believe that their employer is not truly supportive of them in their career advancement, or if they are not satisfied with their job, no amount of training and development will keep them from leaving. In fact, the HR consulting firm, Watson Wyatt, found that the people who just received training are the most likely to leave if they see no immediate means of career advancement with their current employer.[9] We again stress that training and development opportunities must be coupled with corresponding career advancement opportunities.

Getting Started with Providing Training and Development Opportunities

From the above discussion, it follows that employers ought to provide their employees with training and development opportunities. But they should be careful that their investments in the development of their employees don't stop there. Employers should make sure that these training and development opportunities are provided in an environment of real organizational support for its employees. They should make sure that the organizational culture fosters employee satisfaction, or at least does not foster dissatisfaction. They also need to ensure that once trained, their employees have the opportunity to use their new skills in the advancement of their own careers.

In Summary, Offering Training and Development Opportunities Will Reduce Employee Turnover When,

- provided in an environment of perceived organizational support, and
- employee job satisfaction, and
- coupled with internal career advancement opportunities.

Principle 2: Job Specific Training and Development May Reduce Employee Mobility

The Research Evidence

One legitimate fear that managers may have is that they will invest thousands of dollars to increase an employee's knowledge, skills, and abilities without the guarantee that the employee will stick around long enough for the company to earn a return on its investment. Indeed, human capital theory maintains that increases in the training and development of employees' general skills are likely to increase turnover. In contrast, though, proponents of employability policies (policies intended to offer continued employability to employees in return for their loyalty) have shown that offering training and development opportunities that increase employees' general skills may also reduce turnover.[10]

Tuition reimbursement is one of the more popular means of offering general skills development to employees. George Benson and his colleagues analyzed data from over 9400 employees and found that tuition reimbursement actually decreased turnover during the period that employees were taking classes. Interestingly, they also found that employees who took classes via tuition reimbursement programs without earning a degree were actually less likely to quit than employees who did not take advantage of the tuition reimbursement. It was only the employees who earned a degree through tuition reimbursement that were more likely to turnover. Since earning a degree can take several years, and employees are less likely to quit while receiving tuition reimbursement, employers may get the benefit of retaining a more educated employee for quite a while before they graduate. Although employees who did earn degrees through tuition reimbursement were more likely to quit, if they were offered a promotion upon degree completion they were less likely to quit. Taken together, these findings indicate that tuition reimbursement plans can benefit both employees and employers, especially if the employer recognizes and rewards degree earning employees.

One way to increase employees' skills and abilities without increasing their external mobility is to offer less general, job specific training. We say "external mobility" to mean the ease of movement to another firm.

Job specific training, training specific to the procedures and processes of the organization that is not easily transferable to other organizations, can satisfy a valuable employee's desire for career advancement only if there are viable options for internal mobility (mobility within the current employer).

Getting Started with Offering Job Specific Training and Development

Job specific training will reduce turnover only if employees see a direct link between the training and internal career advancement opportunities. Beyond promising advancement upon completion of training, which is viable in some cases, the most common method for communicating internal mobility is through internal job boards. Internal job boards give employees the ability to connect their new skills to new opportunities within the same organization. They also give employees a sense of ownership over their own career. Peter Capelli reports that Dow Chemical reduced turnover by 50% when they implemented an internal job board system.[11] The best internal job board systems: (1) allow all employees to view available jobs; (2) identify the specific knowledge, skills, and abilities necessary to be eligible for the job; (3) give some indication of the pay range and organizational level of the job; and (4) are tied to reasonable tenure requirements (discussed in more detail in the next section) such as number of months an employee must have been with the company or in their current position before they are eligible for transfer.

In Summary, Job Specific Training and Development Can Reduce Turnover By:

- increasing internal mobility,
- without increasing external mobility,
- but should be coupled with
  - a) promises of advancement upon successful completion of training, or an internal job board system, that
    - allows all employees to view available jobs,
    - identifies the specific knowledge, skills, and abilities necessary,

- gives an indication of the pay range and organizational level, and
- is tied to reasonable tenure requirements.

Principle 3: Tying Training and Development to Tenure Can Reduce Turnover

The Research Evidence

Although offering job specific training that increases skills and internal mobility without increasing external mobility is advisable, it is not always doable. When general skills and abilities will be the outcomes, it is wise to tie training and development opportunities to tenure requirements.

As noted earlier, we once worked with a firm on a project that reduced turnover by over 80%. We accomplished this primarily through tying training opportunities to tenure requirements. In researching the turnover problem we found that most of the turnover was within the first 90 days. So we spread what was originally one week of job training over a 6-month period. Employees received basic training within the first week. This allowed them to gain proficiency in the basics of the job. After 90 days on the job and if performance was satisfactory, employees were given the second round of training. This second round of training allowed the employees to be able to handle increased responsibility, along with which came a small increase in pay. Finally, after 180 days on the job and continued satisfactory job performance, employees were given the final round of training, which allowed them to carry out all of the duties of the job. And, you guessed it, successful completion of this training came with another slight increase in pay. This training program resulted in lower turnover because it had the multiple advantages of being job specific training tied to tenure requirements and opportunities for rapid career advancement and pay increases.

Getting Started with Tying Training and Development with Tenure Requirements

Remember to try to make training and development opportunities specific to your organization. When you cannot, tie training and development opportunities to tenure requirements. Or better yet, do both.

In Summary, Tying Training and Development Opportunities to Tenure Requirements:

- can reduce turnover, especially
- when timed with those more troublesome turnover milestones, and
- paired with providing job specific training.

Principle 4: Training Supervisors and Managers May Reduce Turnover at All Levels

The Research Evidence

As discussed earlier in Chapter 5, immediate supervisors and managers play a large role in whether employees will stay or leave their company. Therefore, when you are considering training and development in the context of employee turnover, remember to train supervisors and managers in employee management and leadership skills. Youngsoo Choi and Duncan Dickson found evidence that management training programs lead to increased employee satisfaction and reduced turnover that may offset the monetary investment.[12] Specifically, they found that training managers in human resource management skills such as interviewing techniques, sexual harassment, workforce diversity, and employee performance appraisal, as well as in job specific technical skills reduced turnover in just one year from 89 to 57%.

Getting Started with Training Supervisors and Managers

When training employees, don't forget to train supervisors and managers as well. They play a pivotal role in whether employees decide to leave or stay. Training supervisors and managers in both HR and technical related skills can reduce turnover among the ranks of supervisors, managers, and frontline employees.

In Summary, Training for Supervisors and Managers in HR Management Skills and Job Specific Technical Skills Can Reduce Employee Turnover:

- among the ranks of supervisors and
- managers, as well as
- frontline employees.

CHAPTER 10

Sometimes Pay Does Matter

Compensation, Rewards, and Employee Turnover

We argued in Chapter 2 that emphasizing the role of pay levels and pay satisfaction in understanding turnover decisions can be a misconception that managers turn to too quickly when diagnosing why employees are leaving. However, compensation is about much more than simply the amount in a paycheck. In this chapter we will examine three principles regarding the effective use of compensation and rewards as motivators for retaining key employees. The first principle we will discuss is that, as we saw in Chapter 2, although it is not all about pay, the structure and procedures associated with compensation and rewards can be important motivators of employee performance and retention. The second principle focuses on the importance of fairness in equity in thinking about how compensation and rewards can influence retention. The third principle we will examine in this chapter is that compensation and rewards can be explicitly tied to retention strategies for even greater effectiveness in managing employee turnover.

Principle 1: Compensation Structure and Procedures Matter

The Research Evidence

As discussed in Chapter 2, pay does not drive turnover as much as many managers might think, maybe even less than some of the data might suggest due to the reasons already discussed. As a matter of fact, Robbins and Judge assert that pay tends to correlate with job satisfaction up to an annual salary of about $40,000. Above $40,000, they state that, "there isn't much of a relationship there."[1]

But, this is only part of the story. Think about it. Most of us wouldn't work for our current employer for free. So, of course the amount of pay matters in some cases. Just as Robbins and Judge state above, at lower levels, one's pay is strongly correlated with their job satisfaction. Still, the amount of one's pay remains just part of the picture. In addition to amount, structure, procedures, and type matter, too. Structure refers to the amount of pay dispersion across organizational levels. As the "Occupy Wall Street-ers" and "99 Percent-ers" brought to our attention in 2011, pay dispersion is an increasingly important facet of compensation. It is a fact that since about 1970, the gap between the rich and poor in America has grown substantially.[2] Bloom and Michel have shown that wide gaps between the lowest paid and the highest paid employees increase the likelihood that managers and other employees will voluntarily leave an organization.[3]

Pay procedures refer to the determination and administration of pay levels, raises, and variable pay as well as the actual administration of pay. All things being equal, the level of one's pay, especially in comparison to viable alternatives as perceived by the employee, does make a difference. Pay level may also be seen by some employees as a signal as to how much the organization values them. We will have more to say on this later in the chapter. Suffice it now to say that leading the market in pay for strategically important positions may reduce turnover among key personnel.[4] Margaret Williams and her colleagues found that procedures such as determination and administration of pay raises among other pay procedures can have an effect on employee turnover through employees' perceptions of organizational support. Employees' higher levels of satisfaction with pay procedures are associated with higher perceptions of organizational support, which in turn reduces their likelihood to voluntarily turnover.[5] The way that variable pay is determined matters, too. Variable pay can be briefly described as pay for performance (versus pay for time, or pay for butts in seats). Pay for performance makes sense, and the old adage is true—you get what you pay for. (If you pay for performance, you are likely to get performance. If you pay for butts in seats, you are likely to get just that.) Todd Zenger showed that more valuable employees tend to be attracted to (and stay longer with) firms that closely tie pay to performance while less valuable employees tend to be attracted to (and stay longer with) firms that do not closely tie pay to performance.[6]

Type of pay can also be a strong motivator. "Cash is king" is a common mantra, but it is important to remember, especially in times when cash may be less abundant, that compensation may be made in ways other than cash. Alternatives to cash include stock-based compensation, common benefits such as insurance and retirement plans, and fringe benefits such as the use of company cars, etc. Effective stock-based compensation may include stock options, employee stock purchase plans (ESPPs), and employee stock ownership plans (ESOPs). The idea behind any stock-based compensation is to align employees' interest with that of the stockholders. If they have a sense of ownership, it is likely to translate into a sense of stewardship. Granting employees stock options gives them the option to buy a certain number of shares of company stock at a certain price (the strike price) for a given period of time, usually 5 to 10 years. Ben Dunford and his colleagues have shown that stock options do have an effect on executive turnover.[7] Employee stock purchase plans usually allow employees to purchase a limited number of shares of the company's stock at a reduced rate from fair market value. A variation of this is to allow the employee to purchase a limited number of shares at market value and provide a company "match" in the form of additional shares. ESOPs are also a very effective way to transfer ownership of a firm from the founders to the employees. They are usually tenure-based, salary-based, or both, and they offer tax advantages to the founders (they can diversify their stock portfolios while deferring taxation on capital gains), as well as the company (the contributions may be tax deductible) and its employees (the gains can be deferred under qualified retirement plans). (Of course the authors make no claim of tax advice and encourage the reader to consult their own tax attorneys or accountants for tax advice). In addition to stock-based compensation, the company can also provide common benefits such as insurance and other retirement plans, and fringe benefits such as use of company cars, discount pricing, etc. Nancy Sutton has shown that companies offering higher levels of insurance and retirement benefits generally experience lower levels of employee turnover.[8]

Tailoring the types of rewards to what employees value can increase the impact of rewards on retention. For example, what do top performers value? Of course no two employees are the same, but a 2003 survey by Watson Wyatt revealed the following cash-based reward programs as the five most highly valued programs by the top 10% of employees at 16 US companies: (1) cash-based long-term incentive plans, (2) cash-based short-term incentive bonuses, (3) on the spot cash-based recognition, (4) custom compensation plans, and (5) stock options. The same survey revealed the following as the five most highly valued non cash-based reward programs by the same top 10% of employees: (1) defined contribution retirement plans, (2) advancement opportunities, (3) defined benefit retirement plans, (4) flexible schedules, and (5) career development.[9]

Total reward strategies recognize these compensation and non-compensation based rewards, and Robert Heneman wrote an excellent report for the SHRM foundation describing the components and values of total rewards strategies.[10] Heneman partitions total rewards into compensation (including base pay, merit pay, incentives, promotions, and pay increases), benefits (including health and welfare, paid time off, and retirement), and personal growth (including training, career development, and performance management). Used in tandem and guided by company strategy, these total rewards have employee level positive effects (such as increased productivity and job satisfaction, and decreased employee complaints and turnover) as well as organizational level positive effects (increased revenue and profits, and decreased costs and customer complaints). There is even evidence that too much emphasis on extrinsic rewards (e.g., pay) can stifle the intrinsic motivation that originates within the individual for performing well, having completed a task, or enjoying one's work.[11] Clearly, cash may be king, but a full deck includes many other important cards as well.

Getting Started with Motivating Retention Through Compensation and Rewards

As the foregoing discussion highlights, there is much more to compensating employees for retention than just paying them more money. Level of pay does matter, as do the structure (dispersion) of pay, procedures (determination and administration of levels, raises, and variable pay), and type of pay (whether it is in cash or noncash alternatives). It is important to take a look at each of these aspects of pay in the context of the industry, strategy, and culture of the organization.

In Summary, Managers of Compensation and Rewards Programs Should:

- consider paying some strategic positions above the market rate,
- remember the importance of pay dispersion on employee morale,
- determine and administer compensation and rewards fairly requiring the development of an effective performance management system,
- keep in mind that cash is not the only effective form of compensation, and
- tailor rewards to employee needs and values.

Principle 2: Fairness and Equity Are Important Compensation Considerations

"It's not fair." Managers hear it often. But what do employees mean when they talk about "fair"? How do they calculate what's fair? John Stacy Adams offers his equity theory as an explanation for employees' calculations of fair.[12]

The Research Evidence

According to Adams' equity theory, employees like to know that what they get out of their job as compared to what they put into it is roughly the same as that of what comparable other people get out of and put into their jobs. Employees may compare their input–output ratio to other employees inside the firm or other employees outside the firm. ("I work as hard as her. Why does she make so much more?") They may also compare their ratio to what they experienced previously either inside or outside the firm. ("I thought becoming a manager would have made things so much better, but now that I am a manager, I work twice as many hours for only 15% more.") Finally, employees may compare their input–output ratio to their "ideal selves" (the self that they wish or hope they might be). ("My plan was to have retired by now and live off my savings. But I'm now working harder than ever, paycheck to paycheck.") These different comparison groups (external others, internal others, previous selves, and ideal selves) are what are known as one's referents. This perspective is similar to one of the most influential theories of employee turnover: the theory of organizational equilibrium. A key tenet of this theory is that individuals make the decisions whether to continue participating in an organization based largely on the balance between their perceived contributions to the organization and the perceived inducements offered by the organization in return.[13]

Brian Helshizer found that perceptions of pay equity are significant in managing employee commitment and turnover.[14] Later research corroborated his findings in that reductions in turnover were shown to be a result of reward systems that employees perceive as fair in terms of equity theory.[15]

Getting Started with Generating Perceived Equity in Compensation and Rewards

In determining pay and rewards systems, it is important to consider equity both internally and externally. To ensure external equity, make sure that you know what similar jobs are paid in other similar organizations, for example, through the use of salary surveys. Comparison organizations should be those that your employees could reasonably leave your company for. Make sure that you include geographical cost of living adjustments in your calculations, and that you are comparing similar jobs. Similar job titles are not enough; the job descriptions, duties, and KSAs necessary to perform the jobs, as well as the environment and working conditions should be taken into consideration as well.

To ensure internal equity you will first want to make sure that similar jobs are paid similarly. Beyond this, it is important to establish a fair system for providing merit increases and performance bonuses with clearly described and transparent procedures and standards communicated to all employees. Additionally, you may want to also consider educational and experiential differences among employees as well as geographic differences for cost of living adjustments. All of these determinants should be communicated clearly and honestly to employees so that they know how pay differences in similar positions are determined.

In Summary, to Manage Employees' Perceptions of Pay Equity:

- know what similar jobs are paying in similar organizations,
- pay similar jobs within your organization similarly,
- use objective criteria such as education, experience, performance, and geography to determine pay differences within your company, and
- understand what referents employees use to make their equity calculations,
- clearly communicate standards and procedures used to make pay decisions to all employees.

Principle 3: Linking Compensation and Rewards to Retention May Help Manage Turnover

One final consideration when discussing the use of compensation and rewards in managing employee turnover is linking pay and rewards to tenure milestones. The effective use of this strategy can be very successful in managing employee retention.

The Research Evidence

Studies have shown that many different types of rewards can be linked to tenure requirements and have a positive effect on employee retention. Benefits with relatively long-term vesting schedules such as stock options, ESOPs, and retirement plans have been shown to effectively manage turnover.[16] The idea is that when employees see tangible benefits to remaining loyal over a three to five year period, they are more likely to invest that time with the company. Of course the vesting period should be long enough to provide employee retention benefits for the employer, but short enough as to not make the investment in time commitment seem overwhelming to the employee. Traditional vesting schedules for these types of benefits have been three to five years. Some companies are playing with shorter (two-, or even one-year) vesting schedules.

In addition to the benefits discussed above, with their long-term vesting schedules, other rewards such as performance bonuses, skill-based pay, and even on-the-spot rewards can provide for shorter-term retention management. Most organizations that offer annual performance or profit-based bonus plans have recognized that employees considering leaving will often stay until just after their bonuses are paid out. The balance here is to make sure that bonuses are paid out soon enough after performance for employees to conceptually link the reward to the performance, but to have a long enough stretch of time between bonuses to encourage employee retention. This is a balance that all organizations will have to find based on their own culture and strategy, but quarterly seems to be about as often as necessary while annually is the recommended maximum.

A strategy that combines skill-based pay with training and development opportunities may also help manage turnover. As discussed previously, we once managed a project where the majority of employee turnover in one particular department was within the first 180 days. One of the strategies we used to reduce turnover was to offer base pay raises upon successful completion of training at intervals of 90 and 180 days. Employees who successfully completed training were able to perform more complex tasks, and were therefore provided with a slight pay increase and a promotion. This was very effective in reducing turnover during the first 180 days.

Another creative solution noted by Paula Malone was the use of on-the-spot rewards when employees were "caught" doing a great job. The on-the-spot cash bonuses were effective in providing the conceptual link of the reward to the performance. And to manage retention, employees who received on-the-spot cash rewards were eligible for a $200 quarterly drawing and an annual drawing in which they received public recognition by the top management team.[17]

Getting Started with Linking Compensation and Rewards with Employee Retention

In linking rewards to retention milestones it is a good idea to provide rewards for both long-term (e.g., retirement, stock options, ESOPs) retention goals and short-term (e.g., training and skill-based plans, recognition programs, quarterly semiannual, or annual performance bonuses) retention goals. By laddering different retention-based compensation and rewards programs it may be possible to keep a continuous regiment of payments and anticipation of payments such that retention is continuously encouraged.

In Summary, in Linking Compensation and Rewards to Retention, Consider:

- providing benefits and rewards with long-term vesting schedules,
- providing rewards with shorter-term schedules, and
- laddering retention based rewards programs.

CHAPTER 11

Employees Leave Bosses

Supervision, Leadership, and Employee Turnover

There is a common adage that employees leave supervisors, not companies. Having read this far you can probably guess that the relationship is a bit more complex than the saying would have you believe. It is important for employees to know that they have the support of their immediate supervisor as well as the organization as a whole. In this chapter, we look at the importance of supervisor support in managing employee turnover as well as the role of organizational support. To end the chapter, we take a brief look at the interactive relationship between supervisor support and organizational support in managing employee turnover.

Principle 1: Supervisor Support Is Important for Managing Employee Turnover

The adage asserts that the supervisor is more important than the organization in turnover decisions, so we will start there—with the supervisor. It's a good place personally for us to start, too, as one of the authors once quit a job due to an abusive supervisor, even though he had loved and enjoyed working for the company for four years. Anecdotally, many of us can point to a situation where an employee left a good company due to a bad supervisor. However, what does the research say?

The Research Evidence

Much of the research along these lines—the role played by supervisors in employee quit decisions—looks at the employee's perceptions of the support provided by his or her immediate supervisor. The evidence strongly indicates that support from supervisors plays a major role in employee quit decisions.

In 1997, Karl Aquino and his colleagues asked 150 employees of a large hospital about their satisfaction with their supervisors and this data was later correlated with future voluntary turnover.[1] Their study showed that employees' satisfaction with their immediate supervisors was negatively correlated with thoughts about quitting, and that these thoughts about quitting were positively correlated with actual future quit behavior. Stated more succinctly, they found that employees who were satisfied with their supervisors thought less about quitting and actually quit their jobs less often than those employees unsatisfied with their supervisors.

Three years later, Bennett Tepper found the same perceived supervisor support to turnover relationship in over 700 employees across several companies.[2] He reported that employees who perceived their supervisors as abusive were more likely to quit their jobs than other employees. (Not surprisingly, Tepper also found abusive supervision to be related to lower job satisfaction, greater work–family conflict and stress, and higher levels of psychological stress in general.) In his book entitled *TopGrading*, Bradford Smart points out that the highest performing employees are less tolerant of poor supervisors and are more likely, therefore, to leave an inadequate supervisor.[3] This may be because as top performers they have more options for other employment, or because as a top performer it is frustrating to work under the supervision of an apparently less adequate boss.

Getting Started with Providing Supervisor Support

As a supervisor, there are a few things that you can do to let your employees know that you support them and increase their perceptions of supervisor support. The first is to actually support your employees. But what does this mean? What actions do employees look for in their supervisors as indicators of their support?

To start with, leaders who are physically present among, and available and open to, their employees gain their trust and send a message of their support.[4] Even leaders of virtual and dispersed workgroups can maintain a level of technological presence through Skype, text messaging, email, and such. Beyond being physically present (or technologically present when necessary) and available, employees perceive supervisors as supportive who provide encouraging feedback, fair and flexible work schedules, mentoring and coaching, good task assignments, and recognition for work well done.[5] Finally, sufficient, fair, and just rewards and fair distribution of rewards leads employees to believe that their supervisors are supportive.[6] It is important to note here that high performers are more likely to quit due to insufficient rewards than are mediocre performers and high performers tend to perceive collective reward systems as less fair than individual reward systems.[7]

In Summary, Supervisors Who Support Their Employees Will:

- be physically present, available, and open among employees,
- provide encouraging feedback, fair and flexible work schedules, mentoring and coaching, good task assignments, and appropriate recognition, and
- reward employees sufficiently and fairly for their individual accomplishments.

Principle 2: Organizational Support Is Important for Managing Employee Turnover

The supervisor is only one part of the complex relationship between the employee and the employer. Similar to the idea of supervisor support is organizational support. And employees' perceptions of support from their organizations also play a role in their voluntary turnover decisions.

The Research Evidence

Just as immediate supervisors need to show support for their employees, so do upper level managers and the organization in general.[8] Lynn Shore and Sandy Wayne found in a study of over 380 employees that perceived organizational support (POS) creates within employees feelings of obligation to the organization that manifest in stronger commitment and loyalty to the company.[9] In fact, Anna Erickson and Sally

Blecha report that senior leadership has a greater effect on employee turnover decisions than immediate supervisors. Erickson and Blecha also found evidence that a company signaling support to its employees through its policies, procedures, and employee recognition programs has a greater impact on employee turnover than corporate image and senior leadership.[10]

Getting Started with Providing Organizational Support

Whereas supervisor support is concerned with the employees' perceptions that their immediate supervisors support them, organizational support is more about employees' perceptions that the organization as a whole supports them. Senior level management as well as organizational policies, procedures, and culture can affect levels of organizational support.

For senior management, the list of actions they can take to signal support to employees is similar to the list provided for immediate supervisors in the section above: showing care for, respect of, listening to, and development of individual employees as well as being physically present and open and available to employees.[11] Organizational leaders can also design and implement policies and procedures as well as enact a culture that will foster employees' perceptions of organizational support. Some examples include fairness in merit pay decisions and distributions, especially when considering individual versus group incentives (top performers are often frustrated by group incentives because they feel like they are pulling the weight of others in the group).[12] Even if things at present aren't great in terms of organizational support, senior level management can create a vision for a brighter tomorrow and ensure internal job mobility for high performers to elicit perceptions of greater organizational support in the future.[13]

In Summary, Organizations That Support Their Employees Will:

- show care and respect for employees,
- listen to and develop employees,
- ensure that senior leadership is physically present and available to employees,

- be fair in decisions and distributions of pay and other incentives, and
- provide a vision for a bright future within the organization, including internal job mobility for top performers.

Principle 3: Support From Supervisors and Organizational Support Interact

So which is more important, support from a supervisor or support from the organization? The truth is that there is a complex interactive relationship between them, meaning that effects of one on turnover depend in part on the level of the other. In part, both can supplement for the other and in part, both can be a cause of the other.

The Research Evidence

Tepper has shown that perceptions of organizational justice partially mediate the effect of perceived supervisor support (PSS) on employee voluntary turnover decisions.[14] That is, employees who feel that they have their supervisor's support in turn believe that the organization treats them fairly, thus making them less likely to voluntarily leave the organization. Tepper also found that when internal job mobility is an option to employees, even if they are unhappy with their immediate supervisor, they are less likely to voluntarily quit the organization.[15]

Similarly, when employees identify their supervisors with the organization or when they believe that the organization supports their supervisors, they have a greater sense of organizational support. Employees seem to infer a level of organizational support based on perceptions of supervisor support from their supervisors when their supervisors are perceived to strongly embody the organization as a whole.[16]

Support from supervisors and support from the organization also have a complementing effect on one another. Maertz and colleagues found that in contexts of high organizational support, supervisor support becomes less significant in employee turnover decisions.[17] They also found that high levels of support from one's supervisor may compensate for low levels of support from the organization. They recommend training supervisors in employee engagement and rewarding them for the same. They also recommend that organizations should make efforts to psychologically engage supervisors with the firm based on the finding that when employees feel their supervisors are aligned with and supported by the organization and they feel their supervisors support them personally they are more likely themselves to become engaged with the organization.

Getting Started with Managing the Interaction Among Supervisor and Organizational Support

It is important for organizations to try to create and maintain high levels of both supervisor support and organizational support. It is also important to remember that low levels of one may sometimes be compensated for by high levels of the other. When an organization identifies supervisors with high levels of employee turnover that appear to be related to a lack of supervisor support, the organization should take actions toward training and rewarding the supervisor in employee engagement, and terminating the supervisor if no improvements are made over time. Removing one mediocre supervisor for the benefit of retaining several top performers can be a reasonable proposition.

Maybe the adage should no longer be: "employees leave supervisors, not companies." Perhaps it may be more appropriate to say that: "employees leave supervisors and companies."

In Summary, the Relationship Between Supervisor Support and Organizational Support Means:

- high levels of supervisor support may sometimes compensate for low levels of organizational support;
- high levels of organizational support may sometimes compensate for low levels of supervisor support;
- high levels of both are much more powerful in retaining employees than high levels of just one; and
- organizations should train supervisors in employee engagement, reward them for the same, and remove them when they cannot elicit employee engagement and high levels of supervisor support.

CHAPTER 12

Engaged Employees

Engagement and Employee Turnover

Much of managing employee turnover, and hence much of what we've said thus far can be boiled down to one word—engagement. Engaged employees are less likely to voluntarily turnover than those who are not.

The first principle we will look at in this chapter is that increases in employee engagement can reduce turnover. In the discussion, we will also consider some other benefits of increased employee engagement beyond reduced turnover. From there, we will consider principles to increase employee engagement. The idea is that if employee retention increases through employee engagement, then you need to know how to increase employee engagement. You will see that many of the principles already discussed in previous chapters can increase employee engagement. Moreover, we will offer two additional principles. We will discuss goals and their role in employee engagement, including how to structure goals for maximum employee engagement. We will also cover job enrichment, what it is, how it increases employee engagement, and, of course, how to enrich a given job.

Principle 1: Increases in Employee Engagement Can Help Manage Employee Turnover

Research has supported a negative relationship between employee engagement and voluntary turnover. In other words, there is empirical evidence suggesting that one key in managing employee retention is to engage them in their work and in the organization.

The Research Evidence

In 2004, Wilmar Schaufeli and Arnold Bakker reported finding that employee engagement is associated with reduced employee turnover.[1] Two years later, Alan Saks corroborated Schaufeli and Bakker's research when he also found the same negative relationship between engagement and voluntary employee turnover.[2] In their 2007 & 2008 Global Work Attitudes Report, Watson Wyatt Worldwide reported that engaged employees not only turnover less often, but are also high performers, and that an engaged workforce contributes to an organization's successful financial performance.[3]

In addition to establishing the negative relationship between employee engagement and voluntary employee turnover, research has also unveiled several ways in which employers can improve employee engagement, many of which we've discussed previously. A wealth of empirical evidence has shown that providing employees with proper rewards and recognition (see Chapter 10); fair procedures associated with, and the fair distribution of, rewards and recognition (see Chapter 10); clear communication and guidance from company leadership (see Chapters 10 and 11); as well as employee support at both the supervisor and the organization levels (see Chapter 11) can each foster employee engagement.[4]

Employee engagement builders not yet discussed in this book include specific and challenging goals and enriched job experiences to be discussed in principles 2 and 3 below.

Getting Started with Increasing Employee Engagement

To get started with increasing employee engagement we would first refer you to Chapters 10 and 11 as indicated above. Additionally, we refer you to principles 2 and 3 below.

In Summary, You Can Increase Employee Engagement through:

- providing proper and fair rewards and recognition
  (see Chapter 10),
- providing fair procedures and fair distribution of rewards and
  recognition (see Chapter 10),

- providing clear communication and guidance from leadership (see Chapters 10 and 11),
- providing employee support at both the supervisor and organizational levels (see Chapter 11),
- providing specific and challenging goals (see below), and
- providing an enriched job experience (see below).

Principle 2: Specific and Challenging Goals Can Increase Employee Engagement

Much has been written about the importance of goals to organizational and individual success. The purpose of this section is not to supplant or to recreate what already exists. One of the most successfully used goal-setting methodologies, Management By Objectives (MBO), was popularized by Peter Drucker in 1954. We refer the interested reader to his book, *The Practice of Management,* for an MBO primer.[5]

More relevant here, though, is the role of goals in employee engagement, and the importance of engagement to retention. It is this topic to which we now turn.

The Research Evidence

Edwin Locke and Gary Latham are considered the pioneers in the study of goal setting and motivation. We highly recommend their seminal book entitled *Goal Setting: A Motivational Technique that Works.*[6] Although originally written as a theory of motivation, goal setting done right has since been shown to not only increase employee motivation but also to increase employees' sense of well-being, and to provide employees with a sense of direction and focus. In turn, each of these is related to reductions in employee turnover through engagement.[7] Goal setting done right has been shown to reduce absenteeism (often seen as a lesser version of withdrawal than turnover and hence a proxy measure of likelihood to turnover).[8] The theory of goal setting has been corroborated by dozens of independent studies across a cumulative 40,000+ subjects across several nations and across several occupational fields.[9]

Getting Started with Specific and Challenging Goals

Much of the research on setting goals can be boiled down to five steps in setting goals and six characteristics of well-written goals.[10] The five steps in good goal writing offered by Robbins and Coulter are: (1) Review the organization's mission, or purpose. It is important to be sure that employees are working toward goals that advance the goals of the organization as a whole. (2) Evaluate available resources. Rather than motivating employees, setting and having goals that cannot be met with the given resources can be a huge demotivator. (3) Determine the goals individually or with input from others. If the culture of the organization permits, it is always better to receive input from employees on their own goals. Sometimes, though, the culture or needs of the organization lend themselves more toward goal setting from above. (4) Write down the goals and communicate them to all who need to know. This serves two purposes. First, it creates a sense of accountability to the stakeholders who are aware of and affected by the goals. Second, it serves as a constant reminder that employees can refer back to regarding what it is they are actually trying to accomplish on a daily basis. (5) Review results and whether goals are being met, and provide continuous feedback to help employees monitor where they stand regarding their goals. This helps make sure that things are staying on track and allows for revision of goals upward or downward as necessary. We would also add that some research suggests strict goal setting may work better in more highly routinized work settings.[11]

Along with the five steps to goal setting, Robbins and Coulter also offer the following six characteristics of well-written goals: (1) Written in terms of outcome rather than action—it is important to make sure that employees are motivated and rewarded by outcomes more than by activity. (2) Measurable and quantifiable—this characteristic of a well-written goal makes for a specific target to shoot for, makes the determination of goal accomplishment an objective rather than subjective judgment, and provides a specific benchmark for the fair distribution of rewards as discussed previously. (3) Clear as to a time frame—this ensures that goals are being accomplished in a timely manner that is relevant to the time requirements of the organization. (4) Challenging yet attainable—on one hand employees need to be challenged to sustain a high level of engagement, at the same time though, it is important for employees to believe that they can rise to the challenge given the support and resources provided by the organization. Substantial research shows that setting specific challenging goals is more effective than goals that emphasize "doing your best."[12] (5) Written down and (6) communicated to all necessary organizational members—again these serve two purposes. First, they create a sense of accountability to the stakeholders who are aware of, and affected by the goals. Second, they serve as constant reminders that employees can refer back to regarding what it is they are actually trying to accomplish on a daily basis.

In Summary, Well Crafted Goals Are:

- measurable,
- quantifiable,
- time bound,
- challenging,
- attainable,
- written, and communicated.

Principle 3: Enriched Job Experiences Can Increase Employee Engagement

If Edwin Locke and Gary Latham are the gurus of goal setting, then J. Richard Hackman and Greg Oldham are the gurus of job enrichment. In 1975 Hackman, Oldham, and their colleagues proposed a model of job characteristics that were expected to lead to enriched jobs and, therefore, employee engagement.[13] Specifically, they asserted that increases in skill variety, task identity, task significance, autonomy, and feedback would lead to job enrichment, and that job enrichment would increase employee motivation, satisfaction, quality, and performance as well as decrease absenteeism and turnover.

The Research Evidence

Hackman and Oldham's original study found general support for their theory. The next year, they published two studies that provided additional evidence that enriching jobs through skill variety, task identity, task significance, autonomy, and feedback increased employee engagement.[14]

Getting Started with Enriching the Job Experience for Employees

Based on their theory, Hackman and Oldham set forth the job characteristics model. In it, they showed that increases in core job dimensions such as skill variety (the degree to which a job requires a variety of activities), task identity (the degree to which a job requires the completion of an entire and identifiable outcome), and task significance (the degree to which a job makes an impact on the lives or work of others) could enhance the meaningfulness that employees find in their work. They showed that autonomy (the degree to which a job provides freedom, independence, and discretion) increases the level of responsibility that employees feel for the outcome of their work. Finally, they showed that feedback (the degree of direct and clear information about the effectiveness of one's job performance) would improve an employee's knowledge of the actual results of their work activities. Enriching jobs in these ways, they showed, could lead to higher motivation, performance quality, and work satisfaction and to lower levels of absenteeism and turnover.

In Summary, Management Can Enrich Job Experiences by Providing Additional:

- skill variety,
- task identity,
- task significance,
- autonomy, and
- feedback.

Summary Table. Putting It All Together: Evidence-Based HR Strategies for Managing Employee Turnover

Recruitment

- Providing a realistic job preview (RJP) during recruitment improves retention.
- Employees hired through employee referrals tend to have better retention than those hired through other recruitment sources.

Selection

- Biodata (biographical data) and weighted application blanks (WABs) can be used during the selection process to predict who is most likely to quit.
- Assessing fit with the organization and job during selection improves subsequent retention.

Socialization

- Involve experienced organization insiders as role models, mentors, or trainers.
- Provide new hires with positive feedback as they adapt.
- Structure orientation activities so that groups of new hires experience them together.
- Provide clear information about the stages of the socialization process.

Training and Development

- Offering training and development opportunities generally decreases the desire to leave; this may be particularly critical in certain jobs that require constant skills updating.
- Organizations concerned about losing employees by making them more marketable should consider job-specific training and linking developmental opportunities to tenure.

Compensation and Rewards

- Lead the market for some types of rewards and some positions in ways that fit with business and HR strategy.
- Tailor rewards to individual needs and preferences.
- Promote justice and fairness in pay and reward decisions.
- Explicitly link rewards to retention.

Supervision

- Train supervisors and managers how to lead, how to develop effective relationships with subordinates, and other retention management skills.
- Evaluate supervisors and managers on retention.
- Identify and remove abusive supervisors.

Engagement

- Design jobs to increase meaningfulness, autonomy, variety, and coworker support.
- Hire internally where strategically and practically feasible.
- Provide orientation that communicates how jobs contribute to the organizational mission and helps new hires establish relationships.
- Offer ongoing skills development.
- Consider competency based and pay-for-performance systems.
- Provide challenging goals.
- Provide positive feedback and recognition of all types of contributions.

Source: Adapted with permission from Academy of Management Perspectives.

Conclusion

Talent Emergence

Recent theorizing explores how human resource management practices can create competitive advantage and facilitate organizational performance.[1] This perspective suggests that retaining the talents (i.e., knowledge, skills, abilities, experiences, relationships, attitudes, and motivations) associated with individuals within the organization can lead to the emergence of organization level talent that creates a competitive advantage and can lead to improved organizational performance.

Retaining high quality and emergent talent has been an important concern for leaders in all types of organizations for a long time. We believe that talent management is becoming more important than ever, and that many managers and organizations can benefit from taking an evidence-based perspective to retaining talent. The importance of holding on to valuable employees is increasing for several reasons that we have discussed. Demographic and labor market trends suggest the possibility of shortages of appropriately skilled and educated labor. The nature of work is changing so that employee skill sets can be treated less and less as interchangeable parts and instead performance depends more and more on the unique knowledge, skills, abilities, experiences, relationships, attitudes, and motivations each individual contributes to the workplace. The challenging labor market and organizational efforts to do more with less have built substantial pent-up turnover at risk to leave as soon as opportunities become more plentiful. These trends point to the importance of considering talent emergence.

However, in order for talent to emerge as a source of sustainable competitive advantage, the human resource practices themselves have to add value and the system of practices needs to be appropriate for the context, synergistic, and difficult for competitors to imitate. Our purpose with this book was to provide a foundation for talent emergence based on developing a strategic approach to retention by dispelling common misperceptions about why people leave organizations and replacing them with evidence-based strategies backed by solid theory, research, and peer review. Hopefully, readers are now better prepared to:

- assess the real impact of turnover in their organizations;
- understand what really drives turnover decisions and what leads employees to stay;
- collect and analyze turnover-relevant data and interpret the result through the lens of organizational context; and
- implement retention tools for improved recruitment, selection, on-boarding, training and development, rewards, leadership, and engagement.

Notes

Introduction

1. Manpower (2006).
2. McGregor (2010).
3. Allen, Bryant, and Vardaman (2010).
4. Brittain and Sitkin (1989).
5. Watts (2011).
6. Cascio (2006).
7. Allen, Bryant, and Vardaman (2010).
8. Rousseau (2006).
9. Latham (2011).
10. Briner, Denyer, and Rousseau (2009).
11. Rousseau and Barends (2011).
12. Allen, Bryant, and Vardaman (2010).

Chapter 1

1. Hausknecht and Trevor (2011).
2. Hancock, Allen, Bosco, Pierce, and McDaniel (2012).
3. Griffeth and Hom (2001).
4. Cascio (2002).
5. Dalton, Todor, and Krackhardt (1982).
6. Hancock, Allen, Bosco, Pierce, and McDaniel (2012).
7. Abelson (1987).
8. Maertz and Griffeth (2004).
9. Hom, Mitchell, Lee, and Griffeth (2011).
10. Cascio (2006).
11. Allen, Bryant, and Vardaman (2010).
12. Boudreau and Ramstad (2007).

Chapter 2

1. Bloom and Michel (2002).
2. Allen, Bryant, and Vardaman (2010); Griffeth, Hom, and Gaertner (2000).

3. Mobely (1977).
4. Locke (1976).
5. Meyer and Allen (1991).
6. Graenand Uhl-Bien (1995).
7. Biddle (1986).
8. Allen, Shore, and Griffeth (2003).
9. Mossholder, Settoon, and Henagan (2005).
10. Allen (2006).
11. Mathieu and Zajac (1990); Meyer, Stanley, Herscovitch, and Topolnytsky (2002); Spector (1997).

Chapter 3

1. Griffeth, Hom, and Gaertner (2000).
2. Lee, Mitchell, Holtom, McDaniel, and Hill (1999).
3. Lee and Mitchell (1994).
4. Mitchell, Holtom, and Lee (2001).
5. Mitchell, Holtom, Lee, Sablynski, and Erez (2001).
6. Lee, Mitchell, Sablynski, Burton, and Holtom (2004).
7. Maertz and Griffeth (2004).
8. Maertz and Boyar (2011).
9. Larrick (2009).

Chapter 4

1. Allen, Bryant, and Vardaman (2010).
2. Allen, Bryant, and Vardaman (2010); Allen (2008); Griffeth and Hom (2001); Griffeth, Hom, and Gaertner (2000); Mitchell, Holtom, and Lee (2001); Steel, Griffeth, and Hom (2002).
3. Larrick (2009); Watts (2011).
4. Allen (2008).
5. Griffeth and Hom (2001).
6. Allen (2008); Griffeth and Hom (2001); Heneman and Judge (2006).

Chapter 5

1. Allen, Bryant, and Vardaman (2010).
2. Barber (1998).
3. Allen (2006).
4. Vance (2006).

Chapter 6

1. Schneider (1987).
2. Barber (1998).
3. Phillips (1998).
4. Wanous (1992).
5. Breaugh (1992).
6. Breaugh and Starke (2000).
7. Earnest, Allen, and Landis (2011).
8. CPS Human Resource Services (2011).
9. Colarelli (1984).
10. Phillips (1998).
11. Breaugh and Starke (2000).
12. Breaugh and Starke (2000).
13. Breaugh and Starke (2000).
14. Kirnan, Farley, and Geisinger (1989).
15. Ullman (1966).
16. Breaugh (1992); Quaglieri (1982).
17. Lengel and Daft (1988).
18. Ullman (1966).
19. Hakala (2011); Cascio (2010).

Chapter 7

1. O'Reilly, Chatman, and Barnett (1991).
2. Mitchell, Holtom, and Lee (2001).
3. Kristof-Brown, Zimmerman, and Johnson (2005).
4. Kristof (1996).
5. Lautenschlager and Shaffer (1987).
6. Allen, Bryant, and Vardaman (2010); Fleishman and Berniger (1967); Kircner (1957); Robinson (1972).
7. Hunter and Hunter (1984); Robinson (1972).
8. Mael and Ashforth (1995).
9. Hunter and Hunter (1984).
10. Pursell, Campion, and Gaylord (1980); United States Office of Personnel Management (2008).
11. Graves and Karren (1996).
12. Barrick and Zimmerman (2009).
13. Campion, Pursell, and Brown (1988); Pursell, Campion, and Gaylord (1980); United States Office of Personnel Management (2008).
14. United States Office of Personnel Management (2008).

Chapter 8

1. Allen (2006).
2. Jones (1986); Van Maanen and Schein (1979).
3. Griffeth and Hom (2001).
4. Allen (2006).
5. Feldman (1976).
6. Allen (2006).
7. O'Reilly, Caldwell, and Barnett (1989).
8. Feldman and Brett (1983).
9. Bandura (1991).
10. Feldman (1976).
11. Cable and Parsons (2001).
12. Chatman (1991); Louis (1980).
13. Feldman (1976).
14. Bandura (1991); Feldman and Brett (1983).
15. Jones (1983); Major, Kozlowski, Chao, and Gardner (1995).

Chapter 9

1. Benson (2006); Benson, Finegold, and Mohrman (2004); Capelli (2008).
2. Allen, Bryant, and Vardaman (2010); Bartel (2000); Benson (2006); Benson, Finegold, and Mohrman (2004); Owens (2006); Pajo, Coetzer, and Guenole (2010).
3. Krau (1981).
4. Grossman (2011); Loue (1998); Seikavellas (2002).
5. Grossman (2011).
6. Ito and Brotheridge (2005).
7. Allen, Bryant, and Vardaman (2010).
8. Pajo, Coetzer, and Guenole (2010).
9. Capelli (2008).
10. Benson, Finegold, and Mohrman (2004).
11. Cappelli (2008).
12. Choi and Dickson (2010).

Chapter 10

1. Robbins and Judge (2011).
2. Wikipedia (2012).
3. Bloom and Michel (2002).
4. Allen, Bryant, and Vardaman (2010).

5. Williams, Brower, Ford, Williams, and Carraher (2008).

6. Zenger (1992).

7. Dunford, Oler, and Boudreau (2008).

8. Sutton (1985).

9. Menefee and Murphy (2004).

10. Heneman (2007).

11. Ryan and Deci (2000).

12. Adams (1966).

13. March and Simon (1958).

14. Heshizer (1994).

15. Fay and Thompson (2001).

16. Dunford, Oler, and Boudreau (2008); Sutton (1985).

17. Malone (2010).

Chapter 11

1. Aquino, Griffeth, Allen, and Hom (1997).

2. Tepper (2000).

3. Smart (2005).

4. Erickson and Blecha (2007).

5. Maertz, Griffeth, Campbell, and Allen (2007); Smart (2005).

6. Griffeth, Hom, and Gaertner (2000); Huffman (2005); Tepper (2000).

7. Milkovich and Newman (1999); Williams and Livingstone (1994).

8. Erickson and Blecha (2007).

9. Shore and Wayne (1993).

10. Erickson and Blecha (2007).

11. Erickson and Blecha (2007).

12. Folger and Konovsky (1989); Griffeth, Hom, and Gaertner (2000); Milkovich and Newman (1999); Williams and Livingstone (1994).

13. Aquino, Griffeth, Allen, and Hom (1997); Mobely (1977); Tepper (2000).

14. Tepper (2000).

15. Tepper (2000).

16. Eisenberger, Stinglhamber, Vandenberghe, Sucharski, and Rhoades (2002).

17. Maertz, Griffeth, Campbell, and Allen (2007); Smart (2005).

Chapter 12

1. Schaufeli and Bakker (2004).

2. Saks (2006).

3. Watson Wyatt Worldwide (2007).

4. Allen, Bryant, and Vardaman (2010); Saks (2006); Watson Wyatt Worldwide (2007).
5. Drucker (1954).
6. Locke and Latham (1984).
7. Latham and Locke (2006).
8. Latham and Locke (1979).
9. Locke (2000).
10. Robbins and Coulter (2009).
11. Ordonez, Schweitzer, Galinsky, and Bazerman (2009).
12. Locke and Latham (1990).
13. Hackman and Oldham (1975); Hackman, Oldham, Janson, and Purdy (1975).
14. Hackman and Oldham (1976); Oldham, Hackman, and Pearce (1976).

Conclusion

1. Ployhart and Moliterno (2011).

References

Abelson, M. A. (1987). Examination of avoidable and unavoidable turnover. *Journal of Applied Psychology 72*, 382–386.

Adams, J. S. (1966). Inequity in social exchange. *Advances in Experimental Social Psychology 2*, 267–299.

Allen, D. G. (2006). Do organizational socialization tactics influence newcomer embeddedness and turnover? *Journal of Management 32*, 237–256.

Allen, D. G. (2008). Retaining talent: A guide to analyzing and managing employee turnover. *SHRM Foundation Effective Practice Guidelines Series* (pp. 1–43).

Allen, D. G., Bryant, P. C., & Vardaman, J. M. (2010). Retaining talent: Replacing misconceptions with evidence-based strategies. *Academy of Management Perspectives 24*, 48–64.

Allen, D. G., Shore, L. M., & Griffeth, R. W. (2003). The role of perceived organizational support and supportive human resource practices in the turnover process. *Journal of Management 29*, 99–118.

Aquino, K., Griffeth, R. W., Allen, D. A., & Hom, P. W. (1997). An integration of justice constructs into the turnover process: Test of a referent cognitions model. *Academy of Management Journal 40*, 1208–1227.

Barber, A. E. (1998). *Recruiting employees.* Thousand Oaks, CA: Sage Publications.

Bandura, A. (1991). Social cognitive theory of self-regulation. *Organizational Behavior and Human Decision Processes 50*, 248–287.

Barrick, M. R., & Zimmerman, R. D. (2009). Hiring for retention and performance. *Human Resource Management 48*(2), 183–206.

Bartel, A. R. (2000). Measuring the employer's return on investments in training: Evidence from the literature. *Industrial Relations 39*(3), 502–522.

Benson, G. S. (2006). Employee development, commitment and intention to turnover: A test of employability policies in action. *Human Resource Management Journal 16*(2), 173–192.

Benson, G. S., Finegold, D., & Mohrman, S. A. (2004). You paid for the skills, now keep them: Tuition reimbursement and voluntary turnover. *Academy of Management Journal 47*(3), 315–331.

Biddle, B. J. (1986). Recent developments in role theory. *Annual Review of Sociology 12*, 67–92.

Bloom, M., & Michel, J. G. (2002). The relationships among organizational context, pay dispersion, and managerial turnover. *Academy of Management Journal 45*, 33–42.

Boudreau, J. W., & Ramstad, P. (2007). *Beyond HR: The new science of human capital.* Boston: Harvard Business School Press.

Breaugh, J. A. (1992). *Recruitment: Science and practice.* Boston: PWS-Kent.

Breaugh, J. A., & Starke, M. S. (2000). Research on employee recruitment: So many studies, so many remaining questions. *Journal of Management 26,* 405–435.

Briner, R. B., Denyer, D., & Rousseau, D. M. (2009). Evidence-based management: Concept cleanup time? *Academy of Management Perspectives 23,* 19–32.

Brittain, J., & Sitkin, S. B. (1989). Facts, figures, and organizational decision: Carter racing and quantitative analysis in the organizational behavior classroom. *Organizational Behavior Teaching Review, 14,* 62–81.

Cable, D. M., & Parsons, C. K. (2001). Socialization tactics and person-organization fit. *Personnel Psychology 54,* 1–23.

Campion, M. A., Pursell, E. D., & Brown, B. K. (1988). Structured interviewing: Raising the psychometric properties of the employment interview. *Personnel Psychology 41*(1), 25–42.

Cappelli, P. (2008). Talent management for the twenty-first century. *Harvard Business Review,* 74–81.

Cascio, W. F. (2006). *Managing human resources: Productivity, quality of work life, profits* (7th ed.). Burr Ridge, IL: Irwin/McGraw-Hill.

Cascio, W. F. (2002). Strategies for responsible restructuring. *Academy of Management Executive 16,* 80–91.

Cascio, W. F. (2010). *Managing human resources: Productivity, quality of work life, and profits* (8th ed.). New York, NY: McGraw-Hill.

Chatman, J. A. (1991). Matching people and organizations: Selection and socialization in public accounting firms. *Administrative Science Quarterly 36,* 459–484.

Choi, Y., & Dickson, D. (2010). A case study into the benefits of management training programs: Impacts on hotel employee turnover and satisfaction level. *Journal of Human Resources in Hospitality and Tourism 9,* 103–116.

Colarelli, S. M. (1984). Methods of communication and mediating processes in realistic job previews. *Journal of Applied Psychology 69,* 633–642.

CPS Human Resource Services. (2011). Retrieved June 25, 2011. Found on the net at http://portal.cornerstones4kids.org/stuff/contentmgr/files/decd77a0ea 4ab9d1619839667d1906fd/folder/rjp_phases_1_5.pdf

Dalton, D. R., Todor, W. D., & Krackhardt, D. M. (1982). Turnover overstated: A functional taxonomy. *Academy of Management Review 7,* 117–123.

Dunford, B. B., Oler, D. K., & Boudreau, J. W. (2008). Underwater stock options and voluntary executive turnover: A multidisciplinary perspective integrating behavioral and economic theories. *Personnel Psychology 61,* 687–726.

Drucker, P. F. (1982). *The Practice of Management.* New York: Harper & Row Publishers.

Earnest, D. R., Allen, D. G., & Landis, R. S. (2011). Mechanisms linking realistic job previews with turnover: A meta-analytic path analysis. *Personnel Psychology 64*, 865–897.

Eisenberger, R., Stinglhamber, F., Vandenberghe, C., Sucharski, I. L., & Rhoades, L. (2002). Perceived supervisor support: Contributions to perceived organizational support and employee retention. *Journal of Applied Psychology 87*(3), 565–573.

Erickson, A., & Blecha, S. (2007). *Dear John: A new look at why employees leave.* Found on the Internet at http://www.questarweb.com/htmls/White_Paper_Dear_John.html

Fay, C. H., & Thompson, M. A. (2001). Contextual determinants of reward systems' success: An exploratory study. *Human Resource Management 40*(3), 213–226.

Feldman, D. C. (1976). A practical program for employee socialization. *Organizational Dynamic Autumn*, 64–80.

Feldman, D. C., & Brett, J. M. (1983). Coping with new jobs: A comparative study of new hires and job changers. *Academy of Management Journal 26*, 258–272.

Fleishman, E. A., & Berniger, J. (1967). Using the application blank to reduce office turnover. In E. A. Fleishman (Ed.), *Studies in personnel and industrial psychology* (Rev. Ed.). Homewood, IL: Dorsey Press.

Folger, R., & Konovsky, M. A. (1989). Effects of procedural and distributive justice on reactions to pay-raise decisions. *Academy of Management Journal 32*, 115–130.

Graen, G. B., & Uhl-Bien, M. (1995). The relationship-based approach to leadership: Development of LMX theory of leadership over 25 years: Applying a multi-level, multi-domain perspective. *Leadership Quarterly 6*, 219–247.

Graves, L. M., & Karren, R. J. (1996). The employee selection interview: A fresh look at an old problem. *Human Resource Management 35*(2), 163–180.

Griffeth, R. W., & Hom, P. W. (2001). *Retaining valued employees.* Thousand Oaks, CA: Sage.

Griffeth, R. W., Hom, P. W., & Gaertner, S. (2000). A meta-analysis of antecedents and correlates of employee turnover: Update, moderator tests, and research implications for the next millennium. *Journal of Management 26*, 463–488.

Grossman, R. J. (2011). The care and feeding of high potential employees. *HR Magazine*, 34–39.

Hackman, J. R., & Oldham, G. R. (1975). Development of the job diagnostics survey. *Journal of Applied Psychology 60*(2), 159–170.

Hackman, J. R., & Oldham, G. (1976). Motivation through the design of work: Test of a theory. *Organizational Behavior and Human Performance 16*(2), 250–279.

Hackman, J. R., Oldham, G., Janson, R., & Purdy, K. (1975). A new strategy for job enrichment. *California Management Review 17*(4), 57–71.

Hakala, D. (2011). *The pros and cons of employee-referral programs. HR World.* Retrieved June 25, 2011, from http://www.hrworld.com/features/employee-referral-pros-cons-081208/

Hancock, J. I., Allen, D. G., Bosco, F. A., Pierce, C. A., & McDaniel, K. (2012). Meta-analytic review of employee turnover as a predictor of firm performance. *Journal of Management.* doi:10.1177/0149206311424943

Hausknecht, J. P., & Trevor, C. O. (2011). Collective turnover at the group, unit and organizational levels: Evidence, issues, and implications. *Journal of Management 37*, 352–388.

Heneman, R. L. (2007). Implementing total rewards strategies: A guide to successfully planning and implementing a total rewards system. *Effective Practice Guidelines,* SHRM Foundation, 1–39.

Heneman, H. G., & Judge, T. A. (2006). *Staffing organizations* (5th ed.). Boston, McGraw-Hill Irwin.

Heshizer, B. (1994). The impact of flexible benefits plans on job satisfaction, organizational commitment, and turnover intentions. *Benefits Quarterly 4*, 84–90.

Hom, P. W., Mitchell, T. R., Lee, T. W., & Griffeth, R. W. (2011). Focusing on proximal psychological states and an expanded criterion. *Academy of Management Symposium: Theoretical, Methodological, and Empirical Developments on Turnover and Turnover Intentions.*

Huffman, A. H. (2005). A longitudinal examination of the influence of mentoring on organizational commitment and turnover. *Academy of Management Journal 48*, 158–168.

Hunter, J. E., & Hunter, R. F. (1984). Validity and utility of alternative predictors of job performance. *Psychological Bulletin 1*, 72–98.

Ito, J. K., & Brotheridge, C. M. (2005). Does supporting employees' career adaptability lead to commitment, turnover, or both? *Human Resource Management 44*(1), 5–19.

Jones, G. R. (1983). Psychological orientation and the process of organizational socialization: An interactionist perspective. *Academy of Management Review 8*, 464–474.

Jones, G. R. (1986). Socialization tactics, self-efficacy, and newcomers' adjustments to organizations. *Academy of Management Journal 29*, 262–279.

Kircner, W. K. (1957). Applying the weighted application blank technique to a variety of office jobs. *Journal of Applied Psychology 41*, 206–208.

Kirnan, J. P., Farley, J. A., & Geisinger, K. F. (1989). The relationship between recruiting source, applicant quality, and hire performance: An analysis by sex, ethnicity, and age. *Personnel Psychology 42*, 293–308.

Krau, E. (1981). Turnover analysis and prediction from a career development point of view. *Personnel Psychology 34*, 771–790.

Kristof, A. L. (1996). Person-organization fit: An integrative review of its conceptualizations, measurement, and implications. *Personnel Psychology 49*(1), 1–49.

Kristof-Brown, A. L., Zimmerman, R. D., & Johnson, E. C. (2005). Consequences of individuals' fit at work: A meta-analysis of person-job, person-organization, person-group, and person-supervisor fit. *Personnel Psychology 58*, 281–342.

Larrick, R. P. (2009). Broaden the decision frame to make effective decisions. In E. A. Locke (Ed.), *Handbook of principles of organizational behavior* (pp. 461–480). Malden, MA: Blackwell.

Latham, G. P. (2011). *Becoming the evidence-based manager.* Boston, MA: Davies-Black.

Latham, G. P., & Locke, A. E. (1979). Goal setting: A motivational technique that works. *Organizational Dynamics 8*(2), 68–80.

Latham, G. P., & Locke, E. A. (2006). Enhancing the benefits and overcoming the pitfalls of goal setting. *Organizational Dynamics 35*(4), 332–340.

Lautenschlager, G. L., & Shaffer, G. S. (1987). Reexamining the component stability of Owen's biographical questionnaire. *Journal of Applied Psychology 72*(1), 149–152.

Lee, T. W., & Mitchell, T. R. (1994). An alternative approach: The unfolding model of voluntary employee turnover. *Academy of Management Review 19*, 51–89.

Lee, T. W., Mitchell, T. R., Holtom, B. C., McDaniel, L. S., & Hill, J. W. (1999). The unfolding model of voluntary turnover: A replication and extension. *Academy of Management Journal 42*, 450–462.

Lee, T., Mitchell, T., Sablynski, C., Burton, J., & Holtom, B. (2004). The effect of job embeddedness on organizational citizenship, job performance, volitional absences and voluntary turnover. *Academy of Management Journal 47*, 711–722.

Lengel, R. H., & Daft, R. L. (1988). The selection of communication media as an executive skill. *Academy of Management Executive 1*, 225–232.

Locke, E. A. (1976). The nature and causes of job satisfaction. In M. D. Dunnette (Ed.), *Handbook of industrial and organizational psychology* (pp. 1297–1349). Chicago: Rand-McNally.

Locke, E. A. (2000). *The blackwell handbook of principles of organizational behavior.* Malden, MA: Blackwell Publishing, Limited.

Locke, E. A., & Latham, G. P. (1984). *Goal setting: A motivational technique that works.* Upper Saddle River, NJ: Prentice-Hall.

Locke, E. A., & Latham, G. P. (1990). *A theory of goal setting & task performance.* Englewood Cliffs, NJ, US: Prentice-Hall, Inc.

Loue, T. (1998). Training can reduce employee turnover. *Nations Business 86*, 8.

Louis, M. R. (1980). Surprise and sense making: What newcomers experience in entering unfamiliar organizational settings. *Administrative Science Quarterly 25*, 226–251.

Mael, F. A., & Ashforth, B. E. (1995). Loyal from day one: Biodata, organizational identification, and turnover among newcomers. *Personnel Psychology 48*, 309–333.

Maertz, C. P., & Boyar, S. (2011). Work-family conflict, enrichment, and balance under "levels" and "episodes" approaches. *Journal of Management 37*(1), 68–98.

Maertz, C. P., & Griffeth, R. W. (2004). Eight motivational forces and voluntary turnover: A theoretical synthesis with implications for research. *Journal of Management 30*, 667–683.

Maertz, C. P., Jr., Griffeth, R. W., Campbell, N. S., & Allen, D. G. (2007). The effects of perceived organizational support and perceived supervisor support on employee turnover. *Journal of Organizational Behavior 29*, 1059–1075.

Major, D. A., Kozlowski, S. W., Chao, G. T., & Gardner, P. D. (1995). A longitudinal investigation of newcomer expectations, early socialization outcomes, and the moderating effects of role development factors. *Journal of Applied Psychology 80*, 418–431.

Malone, P. (2010). Training, recognition keep turnover under control. *The HR Specialist: Compensation & Benefits 5*(2), 7.

Manpower (2006). *Confronting the Coming Talent Crunch: What's Next?* Milwaukee, WI, US: Manpower, Inc.

March, J. G., & Simon, H. A. (1958). *Organizations.* New York: Wiley.

McGregor, J. (2010, November). Giving back to your stars. *Fortune*, 53–54.

Mathieu, J. E., & Zajac, D. M. (1990). A review and meta-analysis of the antecedents, correlates, and consequences of organizational commitment. *Psychological Bulletin 108*(2), 171–194.

Menefee, J. A., & Murphy, R. O. (2004). Rewarding and retaining the best: Compensation strategies for top performers. *Benefits Quarterly 20*(3), 13–20.

Meyer, J. P., & Allen, N. J. (1991). A three-component conceptualization of organizational commitment: Some methodological considerations. *Human Resource Management Review 1*, 61–98.

Meyer, J. P., Stanley, D. J., Herscovitch, L., & Topolnytsky, L. (2002). Affective, continuance, and normative commitment to the organization: A meta-analysis of antecedents, correlates, and consequences. *Journal of Vocational Behavior 61*, 20–52.

Milkovich, G. T., & Newman, J. M. (1999). *Compensation* (6th ed.). Homewood, IL: BPI/Irwin.

Mitchell, T. R., Holtom, B. C., & Lee, T. W. (2001). How to keep your best employees: Developing an effective retention policy. *Academy of Management Executive* 15, 96–108.

Mitchell, T. R., Holtom, B. C., Lee, T. W., Sablynski, C. J., & Erez, M. (2001). Why people stay: Using job embeddedness to predict voluntary turnover. *Academy of Management Journal 44*, 1102–1121.

Mobely, W. H. (1977). Intermediate linkages in the relationship between job satisfaction and employee turnover. *Journal of Applied Psychology 62*, 237–240.

Mossholder, K. W., Settoon, R. P., & Henagan, S. C. (2005). A relational perspective on turnover: Examining structural, attitudinal, and behavioral predictors. *Academy of Management Journal 48*, 607–618.

Oldham, G. R., Hackman, J. R., & Pearce, J. L. (1976). Conditions under which employees respond positively to enriched work. *Journal of Applied Psychology 61*(4), 395–403.

O'Reilly, C. A., Caldwell, D. F., & Barnett, W. P. (1989). Work group demography, social integration, and turnover. *Administrative Science Quarterly 34*, 21–37.

O'Reilly, C. A., Chatman, J., & Barnett, W. P. (1991). People and organizational culture: A profile comparison approach to person-organization fit. *Academy of Management Journal 34*, 487–516.

Ordonez, L.D., Schweitzer, M.E., Galinsky, A.D., & Bazerman, M.H. (2009). Goals gone wild: The systematic side effects of overprescribing goal setting. *Academy of Management Perspectives, 23*, 6–16.

Owens, P. L., Jr. (2006). One more reason not to cut your training budget: The relationship between training and organizational outcomes. *Public Personnel Management 35*(2), 163–172.

Pajo, K., Coetzer, A., & Guenole, N. (2010). Formal development opportunities and withdrawal behaviors by employees in small and medium-sized enterprises. *Journal of Small Business Management 48*(3), 281–301.

Phillips, J. M. (1998). Effects of realistic job previews on multiple organizational outcomes: A meta-analysis. *Academy of Management Journal 41*, 673–690.

Ployhart, R. E., & Moliterno, T. P. (2011). Emergence of the human capital resource: A multilevel model. *Academy of Management Review 36*, 127–150.

Pursell, E. D., Campion, M. A., & Gaylord, S. R. (1980). Structured interviewing: Avoiding selection problems. *Personnel Journal 59*(11), 907–912.

Quaglieri, P. L. (1982). A note on variations in recruiting information obtained through different sources. *Journal of Occupational Psychology, 55*, 53–55.

Robbins, S. P., & Coulter, M. (2009). *Management* (10th ed.). Upper Saddle River, NJ: Prentice-Hall.

Robbins, S. P., & Judge, T. A. (2011). *Organizational behavior* (14th ed.). NJ: Prentice-Hall.

Robinson, D. D. (1972). Prediction of clerical turnover in banks by means of a weighted application blank. *Journal of Applied Psychology 56*(3), 282.

Rousseau, D. M. (2006). Presidential address: Is there such a thing as "evidence-based management"? *Academy of Management Review 31*, 256–269.

Rousseau, D. M., & Barends, E. G. R. (2011). Becoming an evidence-based HR practitioner. *Human Resource Management Journal 21*, 221–235.

Ryan, M. R., & Deci, L. E. (2000). Self determination theory and the facilitation of intrinsic motivation, social development, and well being. *American Psychologist 55*(1), 68–78.

Saks, A. M. (2006). Antecedents and consequences of employee engagement. *Journal of Managerial Psychology 21*(7), 600–619.

Schaufeli, W. B., & Bakker, A. B. (2004). Job demands, job resources, and their relationship with burnout and engagement: A multi-sample study. *Journal of Organizational Behavior 25*(3), 293–315.

Schneider, B. (1987). The people make the place. *Personnel Psychology 40*, 437–453.

Seikavellas, M. (2002). Education and training can curb employee turnover. *Multihousing News 37*, 7.

Shore, L. M., & Wayne, S. J. (1993). Commitment and employee behavior: Comparison of affective commitment and continuous commitment with perceived organizational support. *Journal of Applied Psychology 78*(5), 774–780.

Smart, B. D. (2005). *TopGrading: How leading companies win by hiring, coaching, and keeping the best people.* New York, NY: The Penguin Group.

Spector, P. E. (1997). *Job satisfaction: Application, assessment, causes, and consequences.* Thousand Oaks, CA: Sage Publications.

Steel, R. P., Griffeth, R. W., & Hom, P. W. (2002). Practical retention policy for the practical manager. *Academy of Management Executive 16*, 149–161.

Sutton, N. (1985). Do employee benefits reduce labor turnover? *Benefits Quarterly 1*(2), 16–22.

Tepper, B. J. (2000). Consequences of abusive supervision. *Academy of Management Journal 43*(2), 178–190.

Ullman, J. C. (1966). Employee referrals: A prime tool for recruiting workers. *Personnel 43*, 30–35.

United States Office of Personnel Management. (2008). Structured Interviews: A Practical Guide. Web. July 2012. <https://apps.opm.gov/ADT/ContentFiles/SIGuide09.08.08.pdf>.

Van Maanen, J., & Schein, E. H. (1979). Towards a theory of organizational socialization. In B. M. Staw (Ed.), *Research in organizational behavior*, vol. 1 (pp. 209–264). Greenwich, CT: JAI.

Vance, R. J. (2006). *Employee engagement and commitment.* SHRM Foundation.

Wanous, J. P. (1992). *Organizational entry*. Reading, MA: Addison-Wesley.

Watson Wyatt Worldwide. (2007). *Driving employee engagement in a global workforce: 2007/2008 global work attitudes report.*

Watts, D. (2011). *Everything is obvious*. New York: Crown Business.

Wikipedia. (2012). http://en.wikipedia.org/wiki/Economic_inequality.

Williams, M. L., Brower, H. H., Ford, L. R., Williams, L. J., & Carraher, S. M. (2008). A comprehensive model and measure of compensation satisfaction. *Journal of Occupational and Organizational Psychology 81*, 639–668.

Williams, C. R., & Livingstone, L. P. (1994). Another look at the relationship between performance and voluntary turnover. *Academy of Management Journal 37*, 269–298.

Zenger, T. R. (1992). Why do employers only reward extreme performance? Examining the relationships among performance, pay, and turnover. *Administrative Science Quarterly 37*, 198–219.

Index

Announcing the Business Expert Press Digital Library

Concise E-books Business Students Need for Classroom and Research

This book can also be purchased in an e-book collection by your library as

- a one-time purchase,
- that is owned forever,
- allows for simultaneous readers,
- has no restrictions on printing, and
- can be downloaded as PDFs from within the library community.

Our digital library collections are a great solution to beat the rising cost of textbooks. e-books can be loaded into their course management systems or onto student's e-book readers.

The **Business Expert Press** digital libraries are very affordable, with no obligation to buy in future years. For more information, please visit **www.businessexpertpress.com/librarians**. To set up a trial in the United States, please contact **Adam Chesler** at *adam.chesler@businessexpertpress.com* for all other regions, contact **Nicole Lee** at *nicole.lee@igroupnet.com*.

OTHER TITLES IN OUR HUMAN RESOURCE MANAGEMENT AND ORGANIZATIONAL BEHAVIOR COLLECTION

Collection Editors: Jean Phillips and Stan Gully

- *Career Management* by Vijay Sathe
- *Developing Employee Talent to Perform* by Kim Warren
- *Conducting Performance Appraisals* by Michael Gordon and Vernon Miller
- *Culturally Intelligent Leadership: Leading Through Intercultural Interactions* by Mai Moua
- *Letting People Go: The People-Centered Approach to Firing and Laying Off Employees* by Matt Shlosberg
- *Negotiating and Defending Your Margin* by Philippe Korda
- *Cross-Cultural Management* by Veronica Velo
- *How to Coach Individuals, Teams and Organizations to Master Transformational Change: Surfing Tsunamis* by Stephen K. Hacker

CPSIA information can be obtained at www.ICGtesting.com
Printed in the USA
BVOW04s0126070114

340952BV00003BC/5/P